Having reached your 84th year in life - you [...]
many events — Hope you enjoy this book —
Best regards Frieda Bocchino

Wishing you many more years of health and happiness!
Best Wishes — Patti De Simone

Hope you enjoy many hours with this book
    And many more happy years, Andrea [...]
                        to you.

Mr. Akers —
    I have enjoyed the many years working with you and
looking forward to the future years - Glad we can
share this special milestone with you —
                        A friend —
                        Gerene Lord

The Hudson River 1850-1918

A Photographic Portrait

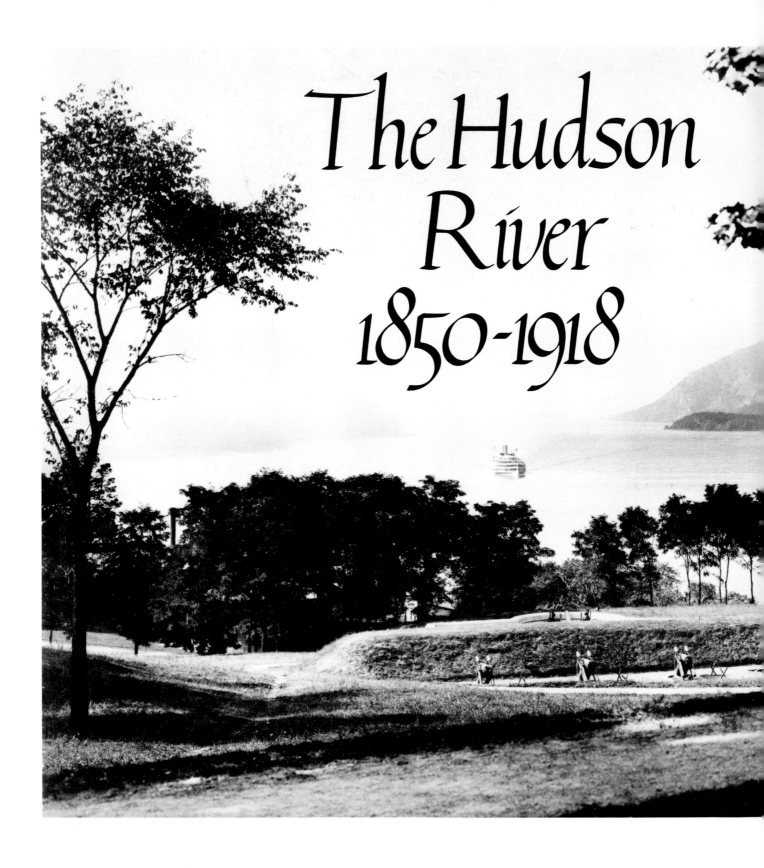

The Hudson River 1850-1918

JEFFREY SIMPSON

A Photographic Portrait

Sleepy Hollow Press

For Clyde and Margaret Simpson

Library of Congress Cataloging in Publication Data

Main entry under title:

The Hudson River, 1850-1918.

  Bibliography: p.
  Includes index.
  1. Hudson River (N.Y. and N.J.) — Description and travel — Views. 2. Hudson Valley (N.Y. and N.J.) — Description and travel — Views. 3. Hudson Valley (N.Y. and N.J.) — Social life and customs — Pictorial works.
I. Simpson, Jeffrey.
F127.H8H78   974.7′3   81-8743
ISBN 0-912882-44-1   AACR2

First Printing

For information, address the publisher:

Sleepy Hollow Press
Sleepy Hollow Restorations, Inc.
Tarrytown, New York 10591

Prepared for Sleepy Hollow Press by:
  Sachem Publications, Inc.
  Guilford, Connecticut 06437

Design by Kirchoff/Wohlberg, Inc.

Manufactured in the United States of America

CONTENTS

Introduction

What is perhaps the first photograph ever taken was not a stiff and formal portrait, such as reposes in the popular imagination, but a scenic view taken from the window of French inventor Nicephore Niepce in 1826. The surviving image shows a stone wall on the left ending in a small turret, another turret on the right, and a courtyard between. Niepce, after experimenting for years with ways to record natural images using light focused on chemically coated plates, succeeded sometime in the early 1820's. His exposures required hours of light, so inanimate views lighted by the brightest sun were the only possible subjects. When Louis Jacques Daguerre, Niepce's latterday collaborator, recorded a sunlit corner of his Paris studio in 1837, there still was no practical way to shorten the exposure time so that the camera could capture a human subject. Daguerre, who developed the first commercial photograph (daguerreotype), improved his technique over the next three years. Collaborators and competitors, including Samuel F. B. Morse, remembered as the inventor of the telegraph, also worked to create a process whereby the silvered glass plate of the daguerreotype would accept an image in less than twenty minutes, and by 1840 they had achieved their end. In the meantime, however, the earliest images to be captured were places: castellated stone walls and towers, artist's props jumbled in a sunny studio corner, Parisian boulevards that are seemingly empty because pedestrians and carriages moved too quickly to be caught.

A reconstruction of the Hudson Valley as it existed from 1850 to 1918 is possible because the desire to record a place, familiar or exotic, survived the technical limitations that defined those first photographs. Even after people entered pictures, the photographs of place—from mountains to Main Street—remained popular.

Technical advances made portraits possible from 1840, and for a while the most fashionable subject for the camera was the formal portrait. By 1853 there were eighty-six portrait galleries in New York City, but scenes of nature and locale continued to be recorded. A series of eight daguerreotypes of the Cincinnati waterfront were taken in 1848, for instance. They could be fitted together to form a panorama of the whole town. The urge to record place for posterity remained steady, paralleling the desire to capture the faces of loved ones.

Between the introduction of Daguerre's process in the late 1830's and George Eastman's invention of the Brownie camera in 1888, the technology of photography experienced several significant developments. The daguerreotype had used a coating of silver and iodine on glass that was sensitive to light. The result was a precisely detailed image on a mirror-like surface. It was a positive image, not a negative from which other prints could be made, and each was therefore unique. W. H. Fox Talbot, an Englishman working about the same time as Daguerre, developed the calotype, a process of printing negative images on transparent paper; these negatives could then be used to print any number of positive images on other pieces of chemically treated paper. This basic negative-positive process is used in photography today.

In the next several decades of the 19th century, the negative-positive process was adapted, improving the image and making it more commercially viable. The most significant development was the glass plate negative, which had to be exposed while the chemicals that made it receptive to light were wet. This necessitated either proximity to the studio or the carrying around of a lot of cumbersome equipment, but the glass plates recorded negative images of such clarity and durability that the collodian process (as it was called) was in use until the turn of the century. Its clumsiness was not a deterrent, and it provided some of the grandest landscape photography ever made. The ambrotype, the tintype, and the carte de visite were other means of making commercial portraits by the collodian process. Stereoscope views were landscapes or posed dramatic scenes that had been photographed twice at angles two and a half inches apart. When viewed through a lens they provided a very realistic three dimensional image. All of these photographs, because they were products of the wet plate negative, remained in the province of the professional photographer or the leisured amateur who could afford the equipment and had the time to tinker with it. Consequently, there were few candid or unselfconscious photographs in the first forty years of photographic history.

Then, in 1880, George Eastman, a bank clerk in Rochester, New York, patented the use of dry gelatin coated paper for negatives, thus paving the way for his own invention, the hand-held Kodak camera that could be used and carried easily by anyone, from schoolgirls to proud new fathers to tourists on excursions. With Eastman's invention, the process of photography became public property. The camera's subjects remained the same—

friends, family, famous people, and *places*—but the style of the images subtly changed.

The evolving technology of the camera is one explanation for the change of image, but there may be other reasons open to subjective interpretation. Informed and inspired by history, the eye does discern certain social patterns. With place a consistent theme in photography, it is possible to draw inferences from how a particular place, like the Hudson Valley, is treated in the various types of photographs, from collodian pictures to snapshots, and what this treatment suggests about the historical orientation of the photographers and the subjects. The earlier photographs of life in the Hudson River Valley tend to be formal in composition, posed, and often static. This formality is in part the result of the cumbersome wet-plate process. But, although the equipment dictated the composition of the photographs, it did not restrict the choice of subject. The grandeur of the Adirondack mountains, the 1889 St. Valentine's Day Flood in Troy, the Great Blizzard of 1888 were all duly recorded. This collision of unwieldy technology with the exuberance of nature appears to inspire the people in the photographs to match the drama of their settings. The lady perched primly in the boat that floats down her own flooded street in Troy, and the Adirondack guide holding himself as grimly as any African who fears that the camera will steal his identity, both seem, in their very self-consciousness, determined to be equal to the occasion. Although this self-consciousness may have been occasioned partly by the camera's demands, it also hints at the determination of the American people to come to terms with their land.

There is an increasing ease in the photographs taken after the introduction of the Kodak, and they tend to suggest a greater assurance about life on the part of their subjects. Vassar girls caper on a class boat ride in 1914, old Van Rensselaer ladies, descendants of the earliest settlers of the valley, laugh into the camera recording their vigil by the night-blooming cereus on the parlor table.

These photographs show the attempt by Americans in the decades after the Civil War to make themselves comfortable with the complete possession of their vast and newly reunified land. Industry and technology—of which the camera itself is an example—provided them with the tools with which to enjoy their home to the fullest. By the turn of the century, as the photographs imply, they had bridged the river, reached for the sky with buildings taller than human beings had ever seen, and were relaxing in the fullness of their home valley, one of the nation's oldest and most varied habitations.

And the camera caught it all.

Rowing serenely on an Adirondack lake beneath a line of high peaks, 19th century visitors seem to have domesticated the wilderness.

Adirondack Headwaters

Adirondack Headwaters

The second half of the 19th century began the age of the professional tourist. Aided by fast ships, railroads, and the telegraph, topee-hatted explorers, scribbling news stories and setting up unwieldy box cameras, penetrated the depths of Africa, climbed to the mountain kingdoms of Asia, and made the trek across the Great Plains of North America. Land that had previously been explored for settlement now was to be explored for the record and measured by the word and the image as well as the mile. John Speke, exploring for the British government, discovered the source of the Nile in 1862; journalist Henry Stanley, in the name of the *New York Herald,* found missionary doctor and explorer David Livingstone in the African jungle in 1871; and photographers T. H. O'Sullivan and William Henry Jackson, accompanying United States government expeditions to explore the Western territories, recorded the first spectacular views of the Rocky Mountains and the Grand Canyon at about the same time. Largely on the basis of Jackson's photographs, Congress made Yellowstone the first U.S. national park in 1871. In the general enthusiasm to chart the earth's surface, territory surprisingly close to home and the centers of civilization was not neglected. In 1872 a young surveyor, employed by the State of New York, climbed the southwest slope of Mount Marcy, the highest peak in New York State, and happened on a pond that he described as "a minute, unpretending tear of the clouds . . . a lonely pool, shivering in the breezes of the mountains and sending its limpid surplus through Feldspar Brook and to the Opalescent River. . . ." The surveyor was Verplanck Colvin and "Lake Tear of the Clouds," his discovery, was the source of the Hudson River.

Lake Tear of the Clouds empties southward only by a slight accident of geography. It lies so near the watershed between the St. Lawrence and the Hudson that a difference of a few miles would have drained its water into the more northern river. Lake Tear is a modest body of water without even any fish—probably because for most of its existence the water of the lake has annually overflowed and been replenished by melting snow during the spring thaws in a process known as "scouring." The ephemeral quality—the sense of being perpetually renewed—that Colvin must have felt when he described the lake as a "minute unpretending tear of the clouds" was also captured in a photograph taken a few years after Colvin's visit by a local photographer, Seneca Ray Stoddard, whose work recorded and interpreted much of the Adirondack and Hudson

Valley territory. In Stoddard's photograph, taken at the time of the spring thaws, the lake appears as a misty basin, seemingly just placed in its primeval setting. In the photographs the lake appears high—at eye level—in the middle of the picture visually embodying Colvin's image of the mountain tear about to fall into the valley. The stream to the left of the photograph might be the nascent Hudson as it looked 65 million years ago, before it carved its channel to the sea.

This photograph is significant because in 1892, exactly twenty years after Colvin discovered Lake Tear of the Clouds, Stoddard showed it as part of a slide lecture to an evening session of the New York State Legislature. The aim of the lecture was to persuade the legislators to pass a bill declaring 6 million acres of the Adirondacks a state park.

Lake Tear of the Clouds, a short walk from the peak of Mount Marcy, perches on the southwest slope of the mountain. Like many Adirondack ponds, it is cold, remote, somewhat bleak, and framed by virgin stands of evergreens. In modern times Lake Tear and Feldspar Brook, its outlet, have been a stopping place for tired hikers.

Verplanck Colvin, discoverer of Lake Tear of the Clouds, surveyed the Adirondacks for twenty–eight years. He described such landscapes as this, photographed by his staff in 1897, with passion: "Elsewhere are mountains more stupendous, more icy and more drear, but none . . . more brightly gemmed or jeweled with innumerable lakes . . ."

There was a new national consciousness in post Civil War America of which Colvin and Stoddard were a part. Having survived the divisive conflict and to some extent having settled across the continent, Americans were wondering just what they had and who they were. In 1869 a golden spike pounded into the joined rails of the Union Pacific and Central Pacific Railroads at Promontory Point, Utah, literally tied the country together with a transcontinental railroad; industry was booming and regular wages lured country boys and girls to the cities to work in the mills. (According to historian Samuel Eliot Morison, "in 1860 the average American

was a landowning yeoman farmer, since 1900 he has been an employee.'') There was an influx of immigrants from Southern and Eastern Europe, an influx that had introduced the threads of very different cultures into the tapestry of national life. This was the ''Gilded Age'' written of by Mark Twain, with undreamed riches for the robber barons of industry and unimaginable poverty for immigrants crowded in city slums. No longer did the North American continent seem to be a land of mythical, infinite potential. For the Puritans of the 17th century, the land had been a clean slate waiting for virtuous inscription by the hand of man; for the American in the first half of the 19th century, the black earth of the midwestern prairies had beckoned like the gold of an Eldorado. But after the Civil War, the prairies became accessible to anyone who could save up train fare. Ownership of 160 acres was possible under the Homestead Act for anyone who would live on it for at least five years. Potential—of the land, of the coal and iron and other resources for industry, and of technology—gave way to the actual. Alexander Graham Bell's telephone was first demonstrated in 1876, and Thomas Edison's light bulb in 1879. The future had arrived, promise seemed to be fulfilled, and Americans looked up, like prairie farmers after harvesting or city storekeepers after a boom year, to see what they had garnered.

In this age of fulfillment, in the three decades following the Civil War, the national quest became as much social and psychological as it was material. The search was for a national identity. The Philadelphia Centennial Exposition of 1876 celebrated the first century of the republic; ''boosterism'' made the citizens of every undeveloped crossroads declare that their town was the equal of the biggest city in the country—if not the great cities of antiquity; and patriotic societies reconstructed the glory of the past of America and gave its present a context. In literature, local colorists such as Sarah Orne Jewett in Maine, Joel Chandler Harris in Georgia, and Bret Harte in California captured the language and customs of different regions of the land, as Washington Irving had done in his writings about the Hudson Valley earlier in the century.

The careful surveying and preserving of vast tracts of unsettled land and the celebrating of various sections of the country in literature were ways of defining just what America was. Another way—which was itself a product of American technology—was taking photographs, such as Seneca Ray Stoddard's of the Adirondacks and the Hudson Valley.

From the days of the earliest transportable cameras in the 1860's, photography played a lively part in creating the American self-image. People saw accurately represented, for the first time in human history, parts of the country beyond their own farm or village. The previously unimaginable expanses of Western deserts—the depths of the Grand Canyon as T. H. O'Sullivan photographed them—as well as exotic customs of Indians and the glories of urban architecture were suddenly available to anyone who could buy a set of stereopticon slides for the parlor. People were dazzled by these photographs, and they became an excellent vehicle for fomenting feelings of patriotism and pride of place. From pride in possessing a photograph, it was only one step to pride in possession of the subject. There were sound economic reasons for starting conservation measures in the Adirondacks, but the bill passed in 1892 to declare the area a state park might never have passed at all—and certainly would never have passed so easily—had Stoddard not spent a year showing the legislators and their constituents the slides of what they, the taxpayers, possessed. In the Adirondacks, in the Hudson Valley, and in much of the rest of America, photography—coming in the last third of the 19th century—not only preserved a record of what was exposed to the camera in that moment but helped to affect the condition of its subjects as we know them today.

The Hudson River Valley had been central in the life of the American nation since before the Revolution, geographically when there were only thirteen colonies, politically during the Revolution when the British and Americans repeatedly battled to control the river, and commercially before the Civil War when it was one of the principal avenues to the West. The photographs of the varied life along the river, taken during the years between the Civil War and World War I, capture moments of transition. The river was no longer as commercially significant as it had been, but the old activities and cultures were still much in evidence. At the same time, the pull of the vast growing city at the river's mouth and the lure of one of the largest wilderness areas in the East at its head created new patterns of life in the valley. Transition in the Adirondacks during the decades after the Civil War saw the region transformed from wilderness to a playground for the affluent, while the lower river came to symbolize America's commercial strength. All of these elements went together to create an image as uniformly American as the technology of the camera and as distinctly varied as any group of individual photographs.

Therefore, the source of the river, Lake Tear of the Clouds, as Seneca Ray Stoddard photographed it on an early spring day when snow still lay on the ground, is a good place to begin examining reflections of America in the late 19th century and early 20th century along the Hudson River and its valley.

Verplanck Colvin's Mission

Although he was only twenty-five years old, Verplanck Colvin had pursued mapping studies of the Adirondacks since he was eighteen and had campaigned relentlessly in Albany for recognition of his work. The legislature, wanting to assess exactly what the state resources were, finally commissioned him in 1872 to do a topographical study of the roiled, lofty peaks of the "Greater Wilderness," as the Adirondack area was known. Colvin set out immediately. In his first year on the project, he slogged through snow ("the snow entered our clothing despite all care, and it was impossible to prevent frequent falls over hidden rocks and tree trunks"), driving his companions and himself ("At length the guides proposed to camp, as night had nearly settled down, but my pedometer had not yet recorded the ten miles at which I had estimated the distance"). It was then that he discovered Lake Tear of the Clouds.

His discovery of the source of the river had more than a sentimental or even topographical interest. It was concern about the river on the part of the somewhat pragmatic conservation lobbies in Albany that had led to Colvin's appointment in the first place. The Hudson and its tributaries were recognized as essential to the state's commercial transportation, and it was becoming apparent that in denuding whole Adirondack mountainsides the lumber industry had affected the watershed and the river drastically. Settlement of the Adirondacks had been late—primarily because commercial navigation of the river north of Albany was impossible—and few had concerned themselves with what went on in the mountains.

The resources of the mountains were being depleted rapidly by trappers, hunters, lumbermen, and miners. The beavers, one of the New World's most valuable resources for the original Dutch settlers, were trapped so extensively that they had virtually disappeared by 1820; the elk had disappeared by 1840; the last panther was killed in the 1870's; and the last indigenous moose was seen in the 1860's. As early as 1813 lumbering was done in the Adirondacks, and two brothers, Alanson and Norman Fox, revolutionized and expedited the lumber business when they sent logs, individually branded for identification rather than linked in unwieldy, laboriously constructed rafts, floating down to the sawmills at Glens Falls. So profitable was this method that the state declared certain rivers to be public highways. In 1850, New York led the

entire United States in the amount of lumber cut and in the 1860's, when a method of making paper pulp from soft wood was perfected, the decimation of the mountainsides was extensive.

While the mountains were being scraped clean of their timber, the earth beneath was being gouged for iron. In the early 19th century more than two hundred iron mines were developed in the area around Tahawus, where the 6-foot-wide Hudson becomes Lake Sanford, before the biggest mine finally failed in 1854 because of the impurity of the iron ore.

Colvin began his mapping treks at a time when many Adirondack hillsides had been cleared and the iron mines abandoned. One of the reasons for his legislative sponsorship may have been the indications of interest in the area for a new purpose, tourism.

The name "Adirondack" was first recorded by state surveyor Ebenezer Emmons in his survey of the mountain region made in 1837. The name comes from a term meaning "tree-eaters" used contemptuously by the Iroquois to describe their enemies the Algonkian, who sometimes came down from Canada and camped out in the mountains. The visits of the Algonkian and Iroquois, who only populated the area during the summers, could have been seen, had there been a colonial observer prescient enough, as a sign of the greatest development the Adirondacks were going to have to absorb: the summer visitor. Harriet Martineau, an English travel writer, visiting the southern fringes of the Adirondacks in 1838, exulted: "What a wealth of beauty is there here for future residents yet unborn!"

The earliest endorsements of the Adirondacks as a vacation area were contained in a *New York Times* editorial on April 9, 1864 that declared land to be a resource worth cherishing in a way that would have been impossible even twenty years before: "Not the least of the advantages offered for residence in our Atlantic cities is their proximity to the most charming natural retreats where we can replenish our fountains of vitality . . . within an easy day's ride of our great city, as steam teaches us to measure distance, is a tract of country fitted to make a Central Park for the world . . . Adirondack is still a realm of mystery. Although the waters of the Hudson, which today mingle with those of the ocean in our harbor, yesterday rippled over its rocks . . . Yet so little has this "wonderful wilderness" been penetrated by enterprise or art that our community is practically ignorant of its enormous capacities.

"Here we venture a suggestion to our citizens. Let them form combinations and, seizing upon the choicest of the Adirondack Mountains, before they are despoiled for their forest, make them grand parks, owned in common. . . ."

On Mount Marcy, at 5,344 feet the highest mountain in New York State, Verplanck Colvin (*left*) and his colleague Blake erected a semi–permanent surveying station from which they could survey the scene northward toward Canada and eastward toward Vermont.

Wilderness vistas, such as this view from the summit of Bald Mountain, attracted the Victorian gentry to the Adirondacks.

But in 1865 another traveler fearfully quavered that if Adirondack beauty were discovered: "We shall have large American hotels everywhere rising like splendid icebergs, suddenly brought down upon us as by the current of travel and migration and sweeping down from the old Arctic of wealth to summer seas of common sympathy and use."

Four years later, in 1869, that very event came about. Thick as a log jam crowding a mountain stream, tourists began flooding the mountains. In the decade following the Civil War there was, initially at least, a new prosperity in an America increasingly industrialized. The population, shifting slowly from the long hours and isolation of farm life to the regular and shorter hours of city schedules, searched for diversions. City folk in the late 1860's were as eager to be led into the wilderness as the Israelites were to be led out of Egypt. In William Murray, also known as "Adirondack Murray," they found their Moses.

The Legacy of Adirondack Murray

336 Raquette Lake Hotel. Open Camp at Night

The Reverend William H. H. Murray was the theatrically handsome young pastor of Boston's fashionable Park Street Church. The church gave him a gentleman's two month vacation, and Murray had spent several summers fishing and camping in the Adirondacks when he published *Adventures in the Wilderness, or Camp-Life in the Adirondacks* in 1869. There had been stirrings of fashionable interest in this accessible wilderness before Murray. In 1851, Benjamin Brandreth, maker of Brandreth's Universal Vege-

Following the publication in April 1869 of the Reverend William Murray's book *Adventures in the Wilderness*, thousands of tourists inundated the Adirondacks. Visitors gathered for entertainment at rough open "camps," that were close to their comfortable hotels.

ADIRONDACK.

Mountain Lake Carry

Copyright 1911 By H.E. Kellogg

Access to the big Adirondack hotels was made easy early on by steam–powered launches known as "carries." The use of the camera—note man on top deck—helped both to popularize the upper Hudson Valley as a tourist attraction and to preserve it by recording images of unspoiled wilderness (right).

table Pills, had bought 25,000 acres for a camp; the then governor of New York State, Horatio Seymour, wrongly claimed to have shot the last moose in the state in 1859; and Henry Wadsworth Longfellow declined in 1858 to go on an Adirondack camping trip with poet James Russell Lowell, Harvard professor Louis Agassiz, and Ralph Waldo Emerson because the dreamy Emerson was taking a gun. ("Someone might get shot!" Longfellow predicted.)

These visits were mere trickles, however, compared to the flood that followed the appearance of Murray's book. It appeared in April 1869, and by June "Murray's Rush" was underway. Thousands poured into the wilderness in response to Murray's promises that ". . . with a guide who knows his business I would undertake to feed a party of twenty the season through and seldom should they sit down to a dinner lacking trout and venison." As for providing the trout, when Murray fished, ". . . *All three were hooked. Three trout, weighing in the aggregate seven pounds, held by a single hair on a nine ounce rod . . . .*" Murray balanced his euphoria with practical discussions of guides, roads of access, supplies, and what ladies should wear ("a net of fine Swiss mull, gathered into the form of a sack or bag, with an elastic clip over the head . . . a pair of buckskin gloves . . . sewed on at the wrist; a short walking dress, with Turkish drawers fastened with a band tightly at the ankle; etc., etc."). Despite the practical directions, however, Murray overreached himself. Paradise itself could scarcely have matched his description and in the black-fly-bitten view of many, Murray's Adirondacks fell far short. The stampede out of the mountains in August was as fast as the flow in. "Liar!" Murray was called. "Murray wrote a reliable book. In it he lies over and over!" But he had only exaggerated, and over the winter the bad memories faded. Enough people returned so that before 1875 Adirondack hotels had increased from fifty to two hundred.

The Blue Mountain House was one of the larger and more barren of the hundred and fifty hotels that sprang up in the Adirondacks between 1869 and 1875. The likelihood of such a phenomenon had been predicted in 1865 by a traveler to the Adirondacks who wrote that if the area became popular "We shall have large Am. Hotels everywhere rising like splendid icebergs . . ."

Stoddard of Glens Falls

While Murray's words and Colvin's measurements were virtually cordoning off and advertising a natural Paradise, Stoddard left his home in Glens Falls—a town just south of the mountains where the first sawmill on the river had been erected in 1753—and began to explore with his camera and box of glass negatives. Stoddard was a passionate advocate of the contemporary Romantic theories about Nature as an elevating force. For Stoddard the Romantic notion of the sublime, in which natural grandeur was thought to be capable of transmuting human thought to its highest level, was realized in the Adirondack ranges, each succeeding the other like lapping waves. He himself noted: "All who love the sublime and majestic in nature of the dainty and beautiful scenery of lake and woodland will find here, within easy reach, a variety which is charming and a peaceful grandeur which must soothe and elevate their weary minds." He wrote books and articles about the region, as well as issuing an annual guidebook called *Adirondacks Illustrated* and publishing a journal called *The Northern Monthly*. In its first issue (March 1906), Stoddard showed his continuing concern for the Hudson in the lead article, "The Question of the Hour: Shall We Safeguard the Sources of the Hudson River."

Stoddard photographed the Adirondacks from the late 1860's until after the turn of the century. He took thousands of photographs that he sold in various formats, including stereoscope views—the duplicate photographic image used in the Victorian parlor contraption called a stereopticon that gave a three-dimensional view of its subject. Although Stoddard also took trips to Europe and the American West with his camera, it was sailing along Lake George in his sloop, *The Wanderer*, that repeatedly inspired his best landscape photographs, in which the distant mountains recede into an ethereal future while the foreground is suspended in the present.

Striped blazers were the height of vacation fashion in the 1880's at the Lake View House on Lake George where the guests posed with a fleet of light, canoe–like Adirondack guide boats—the mountains' answer to the Hudson River sloop.

The embellishments of parasol for the lady and the gilded eagle on the steamer on Lake George convey a decorative image more usually found at resorts further down the river.

Stoddard's luminist photographs were the visual complement to Murray's testaments about the Adirondack region. His stereographs reached thousands of homes, and, in the way of commercial photography even today, the record became the prescription. Mountain retreats that were advertised in photographs as being beautiful tended to be developed and kept beautiful by people who wanted their vacation reality to match the image they had looked at in the parlor back home. The New York *Mail Express* noted in an 1894 article on the Adirondacks: "Close upon the heels of Murray came S. R. Stoddard with his camera, his notebook and his brush, all of which he used continuously to make the fame of the Adirondack Wilderness known to the outside world. Stoddard has done even more than Murray to publish the results of his discoveries for in guidebooks, on his maps, on the lecture platform, on the screen, in poetry and in song, he has for more than a quarter of a century preached the Adirondacks and them glorified."

The Prospect House Hotel, Blue Mountain Lake. The plainness of a hotel's exterior did not preclude the presence of wealthy guests. At one fashionable Adirondack hotel in 1891 room and board were $25.00 per week, and the guest list carried names such as Tiffany, Astor, Stuyvesant, and Biddle.

By 1892, when Stoddard gave his lecture to the state legislature, the effect of his photographs was sufficient to be recognized as a major force in creating the Adirondack State Park. The Albany *Evening Journal* reported of that presentation: "the entertainment was under the direction of the State Forestry Commission (and) the president of that body, Townsend Cox . . . explained that the purpose of the meeting was that a bill might be passed by the Legislature creating an Adirondack Park." On May 20, 1892, the bill was passed. The park that was established covered an area of nearly 6 million acres, within the so-called "Blue Line" (a designation that came about because of the color of the boundary as it is drawn on state maps). The Adirondack Park includes both private and public lands; there were some restrictions placed on the development of private lands and in 1895 the "Forever Wild" clause that was written into the State Constitution prohibited the sale, removal, or destruction of timber in any of the forest preserve areas. (In 1971 the Adirondack Park Agency was established by the New York State legislature to administer more restrictive legislation. The area's wilderness is maintained according to a series of classifications for state and private lands, ranging from "Wilderness"— "where man is a visitor who does not remain"—to moderate development within already settled areas.)

Deliberately rustic architecture and the deliberately rustic term "camp" distinguished Adirondack summer houses. At Bill Dart's camp on Dart's Lake the children of the household were treated to a ride in an ox cart sometime around 1895.

The quality of the photographs taken by Stoddard, Colvin, and others depicting early Adirondack days is that of a series of pastoral tableaux. They are a bit static. (George Eastman did not invent the Brownie until 1888; before that the camera was unwieldy and few "candid" shots were possible.) The visitors, posed on the bows of lake steamers, sitting in an "open" camp with only a roof and back wall for protection, even climbing down a precipice, seem to be posing with a wilderness they are proud of having domesticated. It is Stoddard of course who usually creates the mood but two other photographs that he did not take validate it: one shows a group of guests on the porch of a camp—a conventional farmhouse in this case but built of vertical stripped logs—solemnly contemplating a wagonette full of formally dressed children that is hitched up to an

ox. The scene captured by a Utica photographer named Stratton at Bill Dart's camp on Dart's Lake is as peaceful as it is posed, and brute nature—whether in the form of the ox or in the forest timber—has been harnessed and nailed down. Another photograph of the interior of the Vanderbilts' "Sagamore" (formerly a Durant estate) shows the game room—game as in trophies of the hunt, including stuffed birds suspended from the ceiling and elephants' tusks, and games as in pocket billiards, roulette, and Ping-Pong—contained in walls of rough board, roofed by rafters of log, and heated by a towering rough stone fireplace. The wilderness, the focus of the American imagination and justification for the American myth for two hundred years, had at the headwaters of its most historic river become a national pleasure room.

Despite rustic surroundings, the grandest camps did not stint on amenities. At "Sagamore," owned by Alfred Vanderbilt in the years before his death on the *Lusitania* in 1915, the game room combined games for guests and game as trophies. A stuffed alligator holds a tray of balls for Ping-Pong, a game first popularized in 1902.

The Rustic Rich

Admittedly, it was mostly the rich who appreciated the Adirondacks as a playground in those gilded years between the Civil War and World War I. These were the years when the great industrial fortunes of America were laid. There was no income tax, the railroads reached from coast to coast, and telegraph wires hummed with news of fresh mergers and prosperity. These were also the years of what has been called the Populist Revolt by the farmers whose crops were selling for less and less as railroads could carry more produce more cheaply. But, despite the financial panics of 1873 and 1893, there was usually enough for all. Agriculture and Industry linked well-muscled arms and strode ahead confidently. In Newport, Rhode Island, the rich, resting from their labors in a very plentiful vineyard, erected marble "cottages" that dimmed Old World palaces. In the Adirondacks the palaces—often built of logs and other native materials—were called "camps."

Tiffanys, Astors, Stuyvesants, and Biddles came to the woods, along with the Harrimans and the Vanderbilts. In the 1880's five acres on one of the fashionable Adirondack lakes were sold for $20,000. Winslow Homer painted in the mountains, Mark Twain lounged sardonically, and philosopher William James perhaps found at least one of his "Varieties of Religious Experience" in contemplation of the brooding mountain known as "The Giant" that loomed over his summer home.

Certainly the attitude of the "campers" toward their "Central Park" was not one of staying off the miles of uncharted grass. An advertisement for the Rainbow House Hotel in the 1870's proclaimed: "Here all conventional restraint may be thrown off and all feel thoroughly at home. Connected with the house is a taxidermist's office." The trophies could be captured in an abundance almost matching Murray's original boasts. One hotel register entry noted: "Have been here since the 27th of July. Caught 350 speckled trout, 5 salmon. Shot 17 woodcock, 22 partridges, 2 deer."

Life was calculatedly simple. William West Durant, whose father, Thomas Clark Durant, was one of the builders of the Union Pacific Railroad, tells in his memoirs of life in the camps on Raquette Lake between 1875 and 1925. There were camps belonging to William Strong, a textile magnate who became mayor of New York in 1895, on that lake as well as a $200,000 camp belonging to

Lucy Carnegie, the widow of Andrew's brother. Dr. Arpad Gerster of New York City also lived on Raquette Lake and Durant quotes Dr. Gerster's diary. In 1895, Dr. and Mrs. Gerster paid a twenty-minute call on Phineas T. Lounsbury, the governor of Connecticut, at a neighboring camp. "We paid our last visit in 1893, the Lounsburys returned it in 1894, and now in 1895 we reciprocated . . . we don't come to the woods with the intention of much social entertainment. Some of our neighbors have introduced the American system of gadding about and never being without 'company.' From the first we have declined to be drawn into this vortex of unrest and tedium." However, when the doctor did entertain it was in high pastoral style. The menu for a dinner on August 1, 1897, read: "sorrel soup (sorrel from the patch), cold lake trout with mayonnaise, 2 bottles of Niersteiner Rhine wine, filet de boeuf larded and roasted, little peas, carrots, string beans and potatoes, raspberry ice (berries picked on the patch), coffee, cigars, and Nordhaeuser rye whiskey."

William West Durant, whose father built the Union Pacific Railroad and whose family also sold "Sagamore" to the Vanderbilts, threw up a chalet for himself based on the design of a Swiss music box. He is seen descending the veranda steps of one of his camps.

Guides and Guests

Mitchell Sabattis, a well-known guide at Long Lake, poses with his dog in front of an Adirondack guide boat. The guide boats were as long as 16 feet; they weighed 75 pounds and could be carried by one man. They were made of spruce and pine or cedar, and the brass screws and copper nails used in them gleamed smartly under several coats of varnish.

Occasionally the summer calm was broken by drama more vivid than the splash of an oar in a quiet lake or the crack of a rifle. Theodore Roosevelt, who as a boy compiled a catalogue of birds of the Adirondacks, was visiting again in 1902 when he was Vice President of the United States. He had climbed Mount Marcy and was picnicking near Lake Tear of the Clouds when a messenger arrived with the news that the condition of President McKinley, who had been shot a few days previously, was worsening. Roosevelt decided to spend the night in a lodge near the foot of the mountain and leave the next day for Washington after he was told the President was recovering. Near midnight, however, another message came, saying that the President was dying. T. R. insisted

on getting to the nearest train station. His guides attempted to dissuade him, saying that no horses could find their way along a rutted mountain track in the pitch black forest. Roosevelt said very well, he would walk. Three guides rallied at that and said that they would get the Vice President to the station come hell or high mountains. In fact, the buggy nearly ran off the road several times, but Roosevelt reached a special train at North Creek to find out that McKinley had died at 2 AM and that he was President of the United States. The guide who drove during that change of administration always claimed that there had been "red-hot steam, coming right out of the flanks of that black team of mine."

Tall tales were one of the services of these shrewd native woodsmen who led the summer folk on their camping jaunts and excursions. The guide was the one who knew the paths and trails— sometimes he even blazed them—and it was the guide who directed the campers to the best fishing and hunting grounds, helped set up the camp, cleaned the day's catch, and then entertained with local lore around the campfire. In 1878, Charles Dudley Warner, an essayist and friend of Mark Twain, published an article in *The Atlantic Monthly* called "The Primitive Man." Romanticizing the

An indispensable adjunct to life in the wilderness was the Adirondack guide, first identified in an *Atlantic Monthly* article entitled "The Primitive Man" in 1878. Guides were natives who knew the best fishing pools and hunting grounds and who preserved an attractively crusty independence withal.

wilderness, Warner had written a profile of Orson Schofield Phelps, known in his home territory as "Old Mountain" Phelps because he had blazed the first trail to Mount Marcy in 1849. Phelps, nationally recognized as a character in Warner's essay, lived up to his reputation. Warner had said "His clothes seemed to have been put on him once for all, like the bark of a tree, a long time ago," and Phelps would corroborate the philosophy behind his crustacean appearance saying, "Soap is a thing I hain't no kinder use for." Phelps, who lived to be eighty-five years old, dying in 1905, was the archetypal guide, essential for local color as well as a woodsman's knowledge around every camp. Supposedly the Adirondack guides disappeared because the rich campers spoiled them and turned them into pampered handymen. In fact, the guides did not entirely vanish but their function and the need of vacationers for their services diminished as the upper valley developed. The forest became more manageable, with trails cut and maintained by the state, permanent shelters built for hikers, and mountain-top forest ranger stations to warn of fire.

The guides left one inestimable contribution to water life in the mountains and the Upper Hudson: the Adirondack guideboat. Weighing no more than seventy-five pounds, slender as a canoe and sturdy as a rowboat, the guideboat was built of varnished pine or cedar held together by gleaming brass screws. It rarely tipped over in summer squalls that whipped across the surface of mountain lakes, and one man could portage the boat from one lake to another. The boat was as uniquely an invention of the Hudson watershed as the Hudson River sloop that carried all the river freight downriver from the 17th century until the middle of the 19th century.

Land in the Hudson River Valley has had a history of ownership by the few—which in many cases may have ultimately preserved it for the many. At the time when the Adirondacks were being developed—from after the Civil War until World War I—there was both a pragmatic and a romantic attachment to the American wilderness. The rich who bought up large sections of the mountain land (it was estimated in 1892 that more than one quarter of the Adirondack land was held as preserves by individuals and clubs) helped to maintain an image of what the entire Hudson Valley had once been. At the start of the river, by the limpid depths of Lake Tear of the Clouds, we can imagine it also to be the beginning of recorded history in the valley. The photographer, standing by the tiny lake on a misty day in the 1880's, recorded an image that was unchanged from centuries past, and his image helped to keep the reality from changing.

Thomas Clark Durant, in addition to building the Union Pacific Railroad, in the 1860's, created the Adirondack Railroad running from Saratoga Springs to North Creek so that he could travel to the wilderness in comfort. A train rumbles along the single track of the Adirondack line near North Creek in 1875, beside the still narrow Hudson River (right).

View at Junction of Hudson and Schroon River

As the Hudson River flows down from the Adirondacks it comes into a broad fertile plain north of Glens Falls.

Junction of the Hudson and Schroon

When Albany was photographed in 1869 in one of the panoramic views popular at the time, it was the metropolis of the upper Hudson. Despite a population of 70,000 people and its location at the junction of the Erie Canal and the Hudson, however, it preserved a preindustrial air with its red brick buildings and domed neoclassical State House.

C.S. Rabineau 1869
Photographer

At Home on the River

At Home on the River

Many of the photographic images of life along the Hudson during the decades between the beginning of photography in the 1850's and World War I have a pastoral, idyllic quality that seems to symbolize modern America's happiest notions about that period. There are relatively few photographs of heavy industry—none of whitefaced children suffering in the mills or emerging, stunned with exhaustion, from the depths of a coal mine—and few of the triumph of the machine, such as those taken in the West where giant threshing machines drawn by teams of two dozen horses harvested seemingly endless fields of grain. Instead, in 1869 a photograph of Albany is decorous in red brick and Greek Revival pillars with the dome of the State House and a church spire fronted by a paddle-wheel steamer docked along the river bank. The upper valley's great technical marvel seems to have been the Burden Water Wheel, the largest millwheel in the world at sixty feet in diameter, that was used by the Troy Iron and Nail Company between 1851 and 1896. The industries are essentially domestic: paper mills at Glens Falls, the detachable collar works at Troy, ice cutting in the winter, brick making and Rosendale cement farther down the river. There were festivals commemorating local history: the Hudson-Fulton Festival in 1909 when a replica of Henry Hudson's ship sailed up to Albany to mark the tricentennial of Hudson's own voyage on the *Half Moon* and the voyage in 1807 of Robert Fulton's *Clermont*, the first steamship on the river. As the people sat on porches, played croquet, rowed down the main street of Troy in the Valentine's Day flood of 1889, their delights and disasters appear quiet and predictable, passing in an orderly cycle of seasons, unlike the extravaganzas of change and growth on the frontier or in 20th-century America.

In fact, the suggestion of Hudson Valley life as being orderly and generous is more than an illusory product of quaint period photographs. The Hudson, before the 19th century, was primarily a pastoral river. In the 17th century the Dutch West India Company had granted large estates to landowners known as *patroons* (or patrons) who could claim sixteen miles along the river bank (or eight miles along each bank) if they brought fifty settlers with them. Only the Van Rensselaers at Albany succeeded in establishing a working patroonship, but when the English took over in 1664, they set up manors that functioned in a similar way. The landlord leased land to his tenants—often over many generations—and the tenants

At Luzerne, north of Glens Falls, the domestication of the Hudson began with covered wooden bridges crossing the shallow stream (right).

Unhampered by dams or locks, the upper Hudson flooded regularly every spring when melting snow ran down hillsides that had been cleared of timber. On April 22, 1869, a spring "freshet" demolished the covered bridge at Glens Falls, the town that the timber mills had enriched.

had to pay rents, work a certain number of days annually for the landlord, and contribute poultry, grain, and dairy goods to him. The manor system outlasted the Revolutionary War, and it was not until the 1840's, when a group of farmers revolted in Columbia County, that direct ownership of land became a reality along much of the Hudson. By that time, it was too late for extensive development of the Hudson Valley. With an entire continent stretching beyond the Alleghenies, relatively few farmers were willing to plow fields for the Van Rensselaers, the Livingstons, the Van Cortlandts, and the Philipses. In most of the settlements that were made, life developed along European lines of tradition and continuity, rather than boosterism and competition, as in so many frontier villages. Many of the small towns along the river, from

Glens Falls, Hudson Falls, and Fort Edward at the base of the Adirondacks all the way down to Kingston and Poughkeepsie and then to the Tappan Zee area, more than two hundred miles south of the mountains, were identified with local industries established by the early 19th century. Some of these industries, modernized, continue to be the lifeblood of the towns.

Glens Falls to Troy

In 1860 a Poughkeepsie gentleman named Benson Lossing made a tour that he wrote about in a book called *The Hudson from the Wilderness to the Sea.* Lossing was a shrewd, tolerant, and thorough observer, and his pen sketches, as they were called, provide what amounts to a verbal relief map of the river valley at the height of its 19th-century prosperity. Lossing's group was composed of himself, his wife, and a friend. He refers to them as "Our little company, composed of the minimum in the old prescription for a dinner party—not more than the Muses [i.e. nine] nor less than the Graces [i.e. three] . . ."

A few miles above the city of Glens Falls, the Lossing group described what may be called the beginning of domesticated Hudson: "Between [Jesup's Falls] and Glens Falls, thirteen miles distant by the nearest road, the Hudson makes a grand sweep among lofty and rugged hills of the Luzerne Range, and flows into a sandy plain a few miles above the latter village." The "grand sweep" was known locally as the Big Bend, and in that sandy plain the agricultural Hudson commences.

From Glens Falls to Troy the Hudson meanders through melon fields and pastures, with willows overhanging the stream, looking rather like a 19th-century landscape painting. From Troy to Albany, six miles to the south, the river enters a transition phase, beginning to take on some urban characteristics. The river is spanned by bridges, and just above Albany it is joined by the Mohawk River. The Mohawk, with the parallel Erie Canal, was a major gateway to the West in the 19th century. Because the Hudson becomes deeper here, from Albany south it is an avenue to the ocean, and this junction of ocean and westward routes was one reason that the area became a hub of industry and legislative activity.

Glens Falls, the northern
point of civilization on the
river, was prosperous be-
cause of the lumber industry
and paper mills. The covered
bridge, built in 1842 and
photographed in 1884, stood
until 1900.

Troy and Albany

Troy, six miles north of Albany on the East bank of the Hudson, was the center of the world's shirt collar industry. Photographed in 1870, it had a population of 50,000. The commercial section of Congress Street was overlooked by St. Joseph's Roman Catholic Seminary.

The foundings of Albany and Troy were very different, but the cities were representative of the two strains of American life that mingled in the Hudson Valley. Settlers established Troy in the 1780's, while Albany had been founded in 1624, the same year that Manhattan was settled. Called Fort Orange under the Dutch, who ruled New York until 1664, Albany existed purely as a fur trading center and as a visible symbol to both the colonists and the fre-

DI8818. UNION STATION,TROY, N.Y.

quently hostile Indians of Dutch domination of the valley. Until the completion of the Erie Canal in 1825, Albany remained a small town that served as a market center for the upper valley and central New York State. Even after it grew in population, Albany retained the character of a community that had developed piecemeal. Henry James, visiting in 1904 and 1905, somewhat romantically called it "mellow, medieval" Albany.

Troy was founded by New Englanders, who colonized the upper Hudson in their movement west through New York to Ohio from the late 18th century, and was known during the 19th century as the center of an industry peculiarly illustrative of Yankee know-how. As one admiring chronicler put it: out of every hundred dozen detachable shirt collars made in the world, Troy was responsible for ninety dozen.

The development of the railroad along the banks of the Hudson had been retarded by the steamboat companies who feared competition. Eventually "Commodore" Cornelius Vanderbilt consolidated twelve railroads into the New York Central in the 1870's. Troy's proud Union Station, photographed around the turn of the century, suggests how much the river cities benefited from railroad traffic.

The industries of the Hudson Valley tended to be domestic or supplementary to heavy industry. Rather than railroad building yards or iron foundries, for instance, there were such factories as Westlake's Car Lamp and Lantern Factory at Troy, whose workers were photographed in about 1875.

This industry had started because of a housewife's pique and fatigue. One hot afternoon in 1827, Troy's Hannah Lord Montague, the wife of a respectable shoemaker, decided that she was tired of bending over hot wash tubs scrubbing her husband's shirts, when only the collars were dirty. Innocent of the modern detergent solution to ring-around-the collar, Mrs. Lord snipped the collar off altogether and made copies of it. Now she could wash just the collars and leave the shirts to be worn through their natural course of several days in that era of the once-weekly bath. The Reverend Ebenezer Brown, a retired Methodist clergyman who kept a notions shop, was taken with Mrs. Lord's ingenuity and he commissioned several dozen collars from her. Troy had found its purpose in the world and for just about a century—until the invention of the washing machine made it as easy to wash the whole shirt as part of it—the industry flourished. At its height, there were fifteen thousand employees in more than twenty shirt-collar factories. Many

of these were women, and the New England mill town ideal of a self-supporting, self-respecting proletariat of both sexes bloomed in Troy. A protest against a Congressional proposal to remove the tariff on foreign collars and cuffs in 1893 led to the largest public petition ever presented to Congress to that date: 70,000 names were inscribed in a volume weighing 580 pounds that "four large men" presented to Congress. "It made a profound impression," according to a contemporary report, and the tariff stayed.

Diagonally across the river from Troy with its humming mills and New England sense of purpose, Albany, at the crossroads of

The shirt collar employees gathered about 1880 for the customary group photograph could have worked at any one of the twenty collar factories operating in Troy at that time.

The flourishing state of the Albany Public Market in the summer of 1915 suggests the prevalence of successful fruit and truck farms in the Hudson and Mohawk valleys. According to the sign on the right, the heyday of the good 5¢ cigar had already passed.

upstate New York life, kept something of its old Dutch character. Housewives scrubbed their front steps every day, and church sermons were given in Dutch until after the Revolutionary War. Albany, at the head of navigation for oceangoing vessels from the time of the *Half Moon*'s voyage in 1609, also lay close to the opening through the mountains to the west. The Appalachian chain, stretching from Canada to central Alabama, confined early settlement of America to the Eastern seaboard. One of the few natural openings in the mountains was the valley of the Mohawk, which joins the Hudson just above Albany. Perceived by George Washington just after the Revolutionary War as a natural channel to the West, the Mohawk Valley was finally settled upon in 1817 as the site for a canal linking the Great Lakes, via the Hudson, to the Atlantic Ocean. Ground was first broken in Rome, New York, and

One of the binding facts of small town life was the civic celebration. After the Civil War, America's emerging sense of national identity led to frequent celebrations of the past. Local history galas helped to give citizens a sense of being part of the nation's story. In these events at the New York State Capitol Building in Albany in 1909, the Hudson–Fulton Celebration heralded the three hundred years since the discovery of the river by Henry Hudson and the one hundred and two years since the passage on its waters of the world's first consistently successful steamboat, invented by Robert Fulton.

eight years later Governor DeWitt Clinton in a tumultuous celebration performed "the marriage of the waters," dumping a barrel of Lake Erie water into New York harbor from the very canal boat he had ridden across the state and down the Hudson.

With the completion of the Erie Canal, Albany, always considered the northern outpost of Hudson River trade and civilization, came into its own. When Albany was made the state capital in 1797, it was a sleepy Dutch town of 6,000; when Benson Lossing visited in 1860 there were 70,000 inhabitants. Between two and three million tons of trade annually came in by the canal, while

Entered according to Act of Congress, in the year 1864, by Churchill & Denison, in Clerk's Office of District Court of United States for Northern District of New York.

MILITARY TROPHIES,

IN THREE VIEWS, FROM N. Y. STATE DEPARTMENT OF MILITARY STATISTICS,

Published by Churchill & Dennison, 522 Broadway, Albany, N. Y.

In response to the crisis of the Civil War, society ladies in Albany held a civic bazaar in 1861 for the benefit of the Sanitary Commission, the precursor of the Red Cross. The Sanitary Commission had been created in spite of strong opposition from the Union Army in order to care for the general welfare of the soldiers. Led by prominent public figures, including the landscape archi-

Entered according to Act of Congress, in the year 1864, by Churchill & Denison, in Clerk's Office of District Court of United States for Northern District of New York.

1   2   3   4   5   6   7   8   9

YANKEE BOOTH GROUPE,

AT ARMY RELIEF FAIR, ALBANY, N. Y.

Published by Churchill & Dennison, 522 Broadway, Albany, N. Y.

tect Frederick Law Olmsted, who was secretary, the commission reformed sanitary conditions in army camps, aided cooks and quartermasters with supplies, forwarded packages and mail to the soldiers, and generally assumed responsibilities that in later years would be those of the YMCA and the USO, as well as the Red Cross. One of the commission's responsibilities was nursing care.

Entered according to Act of Congress, in the year 1864, by Churchill & Denison, in Clerk's Office of District Court of United States for Northern District of New York.

SPANISH BOOTH GROUPE,

AT ARMY RELIEF FAIR, ALBANY, N. Y.

Published by Churchill & Denison, 522 Broadway, Albany, N. Y.

Because funding for the Sanitary Commission was entirely private, such charity functions as bazaars were of inestimable worth in providing money. In 1861, when the bazaar was held at the Armory in Albany, the war had not yet assumed the terrible proportions it would later, and the certain antic festivity of the participants in their costumes of many lands and peoples seemed

Indian Bazaar

enjoyable. As photographs these records have an iconographic air: the governmental majesty of the flag-draped hall and the formal, happy solemnity of the American faces in their bizarre get-ups are testaments to the cause. It is almost as though out of what must have been the hurly-burly and confusion of the bazaar itself, the camera picked the sincerity of the participants' intentions.

Anchored in the river, the replica of the *Half Moon* attracted crowds on the shore as well as curious boaters during the official festivities.

In Troy, on the occasion of the Hudson–Fulton Celebration in 1909, the streets were decked with flags and the facade of the Manufacturers' National Bank was graced with a model of the *Half Moon*, Henry Hudson's ship.

H.F. FLEET OCT 8th 1909 ALBANY N.Y.

one million tons of timber, cut at the mills at Glens Falls, were shipped to Albany. After 1851, the year Albany was reached as the northern terminus of the New York and Hudson River Railroad, rail passengers also used that city as the northern point of dispersal for the West. But it was really the canal that transformed valley life, making it a conduit for trade while helping to preserve the unspoiled quality of the valley itself.

The shirt collars made at Troy, the gun factory at Watervliet near Albany, plus the enormous volume of traffic in and out of New York harbor, all were facilitated because the canal provided markets all across New York State and, through the Great Lakes, to the entire Midwest. At the same time, the canal connected the dinner tables of the East to the grain fields of the West. Wheat farmed and flour milled in the Hudson Valley were replaced by the wheat grown more cheaply on level acres to the West and, eventually, the prairies. So, while the Erie Canal expanded the river as an artery of trade and made Albany a commercial hub, it limited the agricultural potential of valley land.

While steamboats replaced sloops and the railroad snaked its way along the shore, while oceangoing steamships sailed up to meet canal barges at Albany loaded with grain harvested by the new McCormick reapers, life along the shore remained sleepy.

Villages retained a 19th-century character, and, as Lossing noted, "all through that region, from Coxsackie to Kingston, the Dutch language is still used in many families."

Albany, pulsing in its commercial prominence on the river, celebrated itself in monumental government buildings such as the Romanesque state capitol, designed by H. H. Richardson and completed in 1899. A noted fin-de-siècle architect, Richardson designed buildings, such as the Boston Public Library, that grounded American culture and law in a medieval tradition suggested by rusticated stone arches. Albany's elm-lined streets of red brick row houses pleasantly surrounded the eminence of the capitol and the grand Gothic railroad station. The city's active commerce was concentrated along the river. There was a huge open-air market that provided farmers in the region with a place to sell their produce and city dwellers with a reliable source of supplies. Public displays, ranging from the somber procession for the funeral of President Ulysses S. Grant to the festive celebration for visitors such as Queen Wilhelmina of Holland, who came in 1909 to mark the tricentennial of Henry Hudson's voyage, called out the populace. In photographs from the period, residents parade around the capitol like members of an opera chorus. Life was comfortable,

The Delaware and Hudson Canal, a section of which was photographed in the 1890's, was begun in 1825, the year the Erie Canal was completed. Together, they made the Hudson a vital trade route between the central East Coast and the interior of the nation.

formal, and, despite the shipping trade, somewhat provincial. The movement of the legislature was no more deliberate than the progress of a Victorian Albany burgher through his substantial seven course mid-day meal.

The Erie Canal, the first big boost to Albany's prosperity, was outmoded by the 1870's, with much of its trade taken by the railroads. In 1905, because water travel was still cheaper than the coal-devouring railroad, new barge canals were proposed, one paralleling the old Erie Canal west to Buffalo, one north, connecting the Hudson River to Lake Champlain and the St. Lawrence River. The canals were completed (after being delayed as funds were deflected to World War I munitions) in 1918 at a cost of $175 million. The canals restored the river as the central artery of commerce. By the end of 1919 river trade had already jumped substantially.

One of the wonders of the upper Hudson Valley was the huge water wheel designed by Henry Burden and built by W. F. Burden in 1851 to provide power for the Troy Iron and Nail Company. Sixty feet in diameter, the water wheel operated until 1896.

Industries Along the River

South from Albany to Newburgh, a distance of more than seventy miles, the Hudson flows around islands created by silt coming down from the Adirondacks and past countryside settled with villages and small cities. On the east bank the cities of Hudson and Poughkeepsie, like Troy, were developed by New Englanders seeking more fertile land and more sheltered harbors than the stony fields and Atlantic shingle that was their portion farther East. These transplanted New Englanders retained their kinship with the sea, however, and Yankee whaling ships sailed down the river from Hudson and Poughkeepsie in the early 19th century in pursuit of whalebone for corsets and oil for parlor lamps.

Concern for the river's resources grew along with a sometimes irresponsible use of them. Stocking the upper river with fish has been practiced for more than a century. This scene from the Fulton Fish Hatchery near the Fulton chain of lakes dates from 1891.

The rather smug prosperity of the Hudson River cities in 1860 was caught by Benson Lossing in a description of his native town of Poughkeepsie: "(Poughkeepsie) is centrally situated between New York, the commercial, and Albany, the political, capital of the state. Its streets are shaded with maple, elm, and acacia trees and their cleanliness is proverbial. . . . The eye and ear are rarely offended by public exhibitions of squalor or vice, while evidences of thrift are seen on every hand."

The careful Dutch housewifery that was reflected in the gleaming brick streets of Poughkeepsie had its counterpart in the husbandry of dairy farming and fruit growing in the valley. Andrew Jackson Downing, an architect and landscape artist who was responsible for the look of many of the Hudson's turreted mansions in the 1840's, also encouraged truck gardening and fruit growing in the valley when the growing and milling of wheat was made obso-

Sturgeon fishing was one of the most profitable of the river's industries. There are two species of the fish in the Hudson: the sea sturgeon that lives in the river until it is grown and then returns to spawn, and the round nosed sturgeon that lives all its life in the river. Sturgeon have been so plentiful and so extensively caught and sold that at one time they were known as "Albany beef."

lete by cheaper flour imported from the West. Fruit growing became a profitable business, and even today apples are exported from around Highland and New Paltz to Europe.

Downing's sense of refined horticulture was so pervasive that it led to his taking action against the pig owners of Newburgh who were letting their animals wander in the public streets rooting out garbage. Downing successfully campaigned to have them restrained and was hailed as "the pig apostle."

The development of truck farms and gardens permitted the continuation of the tradition of good living that had distinguished the valley from the time of the Dutch. On the tables of farmers and townsmen, heirs of the Dutch and English alike, oysters, pea soup, pumpkin bread, and "koojes" (cookies) supplemented main dishes of beef and pork. Among the principal delights of the table and supplementary trades of the river were shad and sturgeon. There were ups and downs in the shad trade, from the plentiful catch of colonial days and the all-time record catch of 4,332,000 pounds in 1889, to the meager catch of 40,173 pounds in 1916. Lossing declared that "the shad is the most important fish of the Hudson, being very delicious as food, and caught in such immense numbers as to make them cheap dishes for the poor man's table . . . (The shad) generally descend the river at the close of May, when they are called Back Shad, and are so lean and almost worthless, that 'thin as a June shad' is a common epithet applied to lean persons." Lossing reported on the sturgeon that leaped like huge sportive dolphins in the river: "The sturgeon is also caught from the Hudson in large numbers at most of the fishing stations. The most important of these are in the vicinity of Hyde Park, a few miles above, and Low Point, a few miles below, the city of Poughkeepsie. These fish are sold in such quantities in Albany, that they have been called in

A stereoscope view from the 1860's entitled "Nooning under the Palisades" shows a somewhat idealized lunch on the river beside a Hudson River sloop, the broad hulled boat that carried commerce and passengers for two hundred years until the steamboat and the railroad rendered it obsolete.

derision, 'Albany beef' and the inhabitants of that ancient town 'Sturgeonites.' They vary in size from two to eight feet in length and in weight from 100 to 450 pounds.''

One of the prominent Hudson light industries was a seasonal by-product of the river itself, ice. In the 1820's, Frederick Tudor, a New Englander, first took a shipload of Massachusetts pond ice, cut during the winter and stored in layers of sawdust in icehouses set deep in the earth, to Cuba, where although half his crop had melted, he made a good profit. After this, Hudson River residents

For nearly a hundred years, from first successful preservation and transportation of ice in the 1820's to the popularization of the refrigerator in the 1920's, ice cutting was one of the river's major industries.

The development of paper made from wood pulp in the 1860's contributed to the deforestation of the Adirondacks. Paper mills were a dominant feature in the upper Hudson Valley by the 1890's when the International Paper Company's mill at Fort Edward was photographed.

decided that townspeople from Albany to Manhattan might quite properly enjoy cool juleps and fresh meat in the summer. By the end of the Civil War the big barnlike icehouses clustered along the west bank of the river north of the Highlands, and from them more than three million tons of ice were shipped downriver every year. The Knickerbocker Ice Company, one of the largest, shipped out 30,000 tons annually until the introduction of the refrigerator in the 1920's ruined the ice business. John Reed, author of *The Hudson River Valley*, interviewed an old ice cutter in 1960: "Icehouse. The old man said he helped cut the last ice in 1919 at Nutten Hook. The icehouse there was 350 feet by 270 feet. Burned down. He was a ploughman but he used to cut ice winters. Good money in it. That last year the ice was 27 inches thick and it had to be brought down to 24 inches by three shavers so it would fit the storage space right. But that was the last of it. One by one the icehouses were torn down or else they burned. Only two left now and they aren't icehouses. Mushrooms.''

The ice cutting in the winter employed many of the same workers, some of them Irish immigrants, who quarried limestone, cement, and clay for bricks out of the river valley hills around Catskill and Kingston in the summer. The limestone, a particular kind called bluestone, with a misty silver-blue cast to its cut surface, was thought to be harder and more durable than New England stone. It was used for Manhattan sidewalks because it would not crack with the cold or, as the Hudson River historian Carl Carmer put it, every time "the boys build a decent election bonfire." Rosendale cement, quarried out of the hills near Kingston, was known throughout the world in the 19th and early 20th centuries. The cement deposit was discovered in 1825 with the digging for the Delaware and Hudson Canal across Ulster County. The cement was heavy and slow to set, but as durable as granite. It was used in the Brooklyn Bridge, the Croton Aqueduct, and the base of the Statue of Liberty. Around 1900, Portland cement, which was much faster drying, took away the Rosendale market, although after World War I, the Rosendale business was revived when repairs were needed on buildings built with Rosendale and the quarries were reopened to get the original material.

Bricks were made from Hudson blue clay from the 1830's until the 1930's. The work was seasonal in the days before World War I because the bricks had to be dried in the sun for weeks before they could be fired. After World War I, with modern methods of drying bricks before firing, the brickmaking could continue throughout the year, and as many as 300 million bricks would float down the Hudson on barges each year.

The industries of the Hudson—cement and brickmaking, dairy farming, fruit growing, and fishing—were the industries of a primarily rural region with access to urban markets where the goods would be used immediately. The valley had no five-hundred-acre wheat farms that would have their produce transported over thousands of miles of rail to vast grain depots, nor hundreds of head of cattle being driven to the slaughterhouses. There was no heavy mining to provide the coal needed to produce iron and steel. The products of the Hudson Valley fed itself and its cities; it built houses and sidewalks and contributed to monuments. The river remained a vital trade route to the North and West.

Small Town Life

Embodying the ideals of contemporaneous painters, Seneca Ray Stoddard's photograph of the lower Hudson shows a human being made small in comparison to the stretches of light–infused landscape.

As the 19th century passed, painters such as Thomas Cole and Frederic Church made the Hudson Valley famous by celebrating it in art. The Hudson River School of painters provided patrons with one of the first coherent styles of painting in America. The paintings were grandiose set pieces, usually of Hudson Valley scenes, that displayed the beauties of nature and suggested America's confidence in its future and the radiance of the land in the Hudson Valley. The vision of a brilliant landscape, suffused with light, testified to the grandeur of nature and the promise of America that was shared by photographers such as Seneca Ray Stoddard. The study of nature as exemplary was, to some extent, possible only in the East, because in the East nature, however awesome, was conquered and contained. Its limit, unlike that of the prairie or the peaks of the Rockies, was known. Its study was particularly appropriate in the Hudson Valley, where there was such a variety: rugged mountains, quiet flood plains, broad surfaces of almost still water, and rushing streams.

This was the quality that made the Hudson Valley in the latter years of the 19th century seem almost like a stage set. Everything was carried out in miniature: the farms were truck farms and fruit farms, the limits of the remaining wilderness (below Albany at least) were known, and, increasingly in the lower valley, the towns and estates were not self-supporting communities and landholdings but suburbs and vacation homes for New Yorkers. Andrew Jackson Downing, responsible for so much of the agricultural character and the architectural look of the Hudson Valley, was also one

The varied topography of the Hudson Valley appealed to 19th century naturalist John Burroughs, who felt that on the Hudson he was at the center of the world. Here he is photographed near his woodland retreat, "Slabsides," located between Coxsackie and Catskill, engaged in wooing some frogs with a feather on a stick.

MEDICINES, BOOKS, STATIONERY,
TS, OILS &c. PIANOS, ORGANS, MUSIC &c.

VAN KENBURGH & BROWN

SLEE BROS., PHOTOGRAPERS, PO'KEEPSIE, N.Y.

The pastoral bustle of Hudson River towns like Poughkeepsie, where the hotel with its line of hacks for hire was the center of activity, was still evident in the 1860's.

Small town consumer businesses provided the commercial life of Main Streets all across the country. Differences were provided by regional commodities such as oysters. Hall's Oyster House in Saratoga would have been patronized primarily by men who downed their oysters with a ginger ale or a lemon sour and then enjoyed one of Hall's imported cigars afterwards.

of the first Americans to articulate the concept of the suburb. Downing proposed that planned communities in "parklike" surroundings be established where successful citizens who had labored all day in commerce could retire to natural but cultivated countryside. Downing's theories, developed in the late 1840's, just preceded the actual establishment of New York City's Central Park and a *New York Times* editorial of 1864 in which the suggestion was made that the Adirondacks be thought of as a giant rural Central Park. The idea of the landscape as morally uplifting and decorative, instead of an adversary to be fought and conquered, could only have come in a settled part of the country after America's boundaries were defined. On the frontier there were great riches to be gained—but the dragons of impenetrable forests, in-

Looking like every main street, Market Street in Red Hook already had a gasoline station when it was photographed around 1910 (left).

The idea that small towns took care of you from cradle to grave is borne out by the services offered by G. A. Cunley's Monumental Marble and Granite Works in North Tarrytown about 1875 (below).

Beer, looked on more and more suspiciously by the middle class as the decades progressed toward the enforcement of Prohibition in 1919, remained the solace of the poor. Temperance was a lost cause among urban and rural poor for whom a "growler"—or pitcher of beer—might be the most pleasurable and nutritious part of a meal.

sects, hostile natives, and drought had to be slain first. There was no distance from nature on the frontier, and if you paused to appreciate it, you might well be overtaken by a blizzard or dust storm or be ambushed.

The Hudson, however, with its settled way of life and colorful traditions, provided the perfect piece of nature for observation. Furthermore, the fact that the river was primarily an avenue of communication between East and West, between downstate harbor and metropolis and upstate forest and farm, meant that its shores were seen by many as a passing pageant. Unlike the Mississippi or the Ohio, where the plantations and cities along the shores were as vital to its commerce as the cities at the mouth or point of origin, the Hudson was, commercially speaking (and in America commerce has always come first), the shortest distance between two important points. From the earliest days, when the beaver pelts brought by the Indians to Fort Orange, later the site of Albany, were the brown gold of New Netherlands, traffic on the river was more important than life along the shore. And this background, domestic quality to Hudson River shore life permitted a grace and decorative distance, whether seen from the deck of a Hudson River dayline steamer or through the lens of a camera.

66

Despite a consistent level of prosperity in the Hudson Valley, there were always people who had to eke out a living on the fringe of local industry. In 1897 women in Glens Falls gleaned fuel from the refuse around the Jointa Lime Kilns (left).

The best known native fish in the Hudson is the shad, which are born in the Hudson, mature in the Atlantic Ocean, and return to the river each spring to spawn. Some of the peak shad fishing years were between 1889 and 1900. When John Silva's shad fishing station on Staten Island was photographed in about 1895 (below), with the owner holding one of his catch, it was part of a very prosperous enterprise.

In the great blizzard of 1888 the Saratoga Fire Department Hose Company turned out their apparatus on runners and passed in front of the Grand Union Hotel.

Several factors contributed to the growth of suburban villages on the lower Hudson. The railroad meant that commuting between Manhattan and a rural home could be a daily reality, and the increased artistic appreciation of nature as an elevating force in the 1850's made nature—in the form of suburban villas—fashionable. Finally, the increased mercantile development of Manhattan simply made it a less pleasant place to live. Benson Lossing in his travels in 1860 lamented that "All of old New York has been converted into one vast business mart, and there are very few respectable residences within a mile of the Battery." This progress would move inexorably up the island, replacing fields with rows of brick, brick with brownstone, and brownstone with concrete. Concurrent with the building up of Manhattan, Lossing noted that north of the city, "fine mansions and villa residences are seen on every side, where, only a few years ago good taste was continually offended by uncouth farmhouses, built for utility only without a single thought of harmony or beauty." Washington Irving was in the vanguard of using the countryside for pleasure and making a country home that was not part of a farm or landed estate, when he

"The Blizzard of '88," which occurred in March 1888, left these banks of snow in front of Albany's Leland Opera House.

enlarged a farmhouse in Tarrytown that he bought in 1835 into the whimsical and charming Sunnyside. When Lossing visited Sunnyside, not long after Irving's death in 1859, he found that "close by Sunnyside is one of those marvelous villages with which America abounds: it has sprung not unlike a mushroom and bears the name of Irvington in complement to the late master of Sunnyside. A dozen years ago not a solitary house was there excepting that of . . . the farmer who owned the land."

In the semi-rural Hudson of the 19th century weather was a daily significant force. On St. Valentine's Day, 1886, the Hudson overflowed its banks into the streets of Troy, and some citizens were photographed rather calmly rowing on First Street.

The first decade of the 20th century was the heyday of the interurban trolley car. The first car on the Putnam and Westchester Trolley Road on March 23, 1907, was decorated to beat the band.

For both farmer and villa dweller along the river amusements and duties were tied closely to the seasons. As cutting ice on the river in the winter augmented a farmer's summer work in his fields, so the pleasure of iceboat racing and sleigh riding on the frozen river took over from the pleasures of shoreside picnics, bicycle races, and circus visits. Edgar Mayhew Bacon, reminiscing about the pleasures of the frozen river in 1907, declared: "Still the ice-decked river is the scene of many a winter carnival. Horses of

The celebration of the nation's centennial in 1876 was a marker in American history that demanded recognition in every town. In Glens Falls they decorated the fire company's hosecart (right) with a model of the ship *Dartmouth*.

The "sweetness and placidity" of life along the river was varied by seasonal pleasures and disasters. In the summer the Barnum and Bailey Circus came to Albany, and small boys ran through the street beside the parade of wondrous elephants.

famous pedigree, sharp-shod and with nerves tingling in an atmosphere like an electric bath, have literally flung distance to the winds over those crystal courses where in summer the boats tack lazily from shore to shore.'' In the spring there were shadbakes when the fish were running upriver to spawn, and responsible

Bicycles were known in some form in the United States as early as the 1860's, but it was not until the invention of the "safety" bicycle in the 1880's with its low wheels and airfilled tires that riding became a national fad. The Yonkers Canoe and Bicycle Club (above), photographed in the early 1890's, still featured a "boneshaker," so–called because of its iron tires on its big and little wheels. The League of American Wheelmen bicycle club (right, top) festooned their meeting hall with Japanese lanterns, things Oriental being another craze of the 1880's and 1890's. New York City police inspector George Lieber perched his wife on a "safety" bicycle at Hyde Park (right, bottom).

The rituals associated with small town civic organizations and clubs helped to punctuate the days and years when tranquility threatened to turn into monotony. The Greenwich, New York, chapter of Odd Fellows turned out their club band with due pomp for the photographer in 1905 (left).

Morris Abraham
age 65 White German
Peddler 14 East Broadway N.Y.
Burglary 3 degree & Grand
Larceny. Stealing a
quantity of silverware
from C. C. Smith
Held to await the
action of the grand Jury.

The fire company, an important organization in communities of wooden houses heated by open fires and iron stoves, also functioned as a club. The pride of the Hose Division of the Middle Falls, New York, Fire Company was evident when it was photographed in 1882 (left). The men had just won a contest against the Greenwich, New York, hose company.

Harrison Dickson
alias
Michael Clarin
Murderer

75.0.458 ⅞

1 # 5

Photography aided the maintenance of law and order with "mug shots" kept on file by police departments. In 1897 the Yonkers police had portrait records of criminals with their misdeeds and aliases listed, including thief Morris Abraham (top) and murderer Harrison Dickson (bottom).

Lewis Fisher
Pick Pocket

The Yonkers files of 1897
also recorded the faces of
Lewis Fisher (right), a pick-
pocket, and Nora Mulcahey
(below), a dishonest servant.

Nora Mulcahey
dishonest servant

192

citizens marked their sense of the season by having shad and bacon for breakfast every morning between April 1 and mid-June.

In much of America between the Civil War and World War I the countryside was deserted for the city but it was the Hudson's fortunate position, geographical, historical, and social, to be a countryside sheltered between cities. Albany, at the river's top and New York at the bottom kept the river, with all its natural grandeur, rich traditions, and good soil, from falling into eclipse, as happened to the countryside of New England and the South. The estates built by new industrialists in the Hudson Valley and the suburbs settled by ex-urbanites complemented the old manorial holdings and the pre-Revolutionary War villages that already existed. The nostalgic image of the river as the perfect rural America of memory was as accurate in fact as it seems to have been in the camera's eye.

Resplendent on horseback and in direct contrast to the stark "mug shots," a Yonkers constable proudly poses in 1897.

142. The Hudson River—Entrance to Highlands, from Cold Spring.

Entrance to the Highlands

At Cold Spring, the Highlands loom above the river today, as they did when Seneca Ray Stoddard photographed them in the 1880's (preceding page).

The institutions, civil and military, that were founded along the river tended to be innovative for their time and also very formal. Both characteristics—the adventuresome spirit and the decorum—were typical of 19th century life. West Point cadets (right) line up in front of their barracks in 1898 in ranks that seem scarcely less architectural than the building itself.

Resorts and Institutions

Resorts and Institutions

The Hudson Valley was a cultural—as well as geographical—middle ground where New England interest in the ideal and Dutch interest in the practical met. The institutions that grew up along the river reflected a uniquely American attempt to make good neighbors of God and Mammon. Religious communes where Shakers awaited the end of the world while shrewdly amassing the world's goods; health resorts where the appeal of the sulfur springs was enhanced by gaming tables; Vassar, one of the world's first women's colleges, where high culture conferred high class; and Sing Sing, the famous prison where the punishing lock step echoed the drill step at the United States Military Academy across the river, all shared the valley.

All of these institutions grew up after 1800, after the establishment of the new United States government, but their foundations were laid in the colonial period. Dutch pragmatism and the sparse

The Hudson River Highlands seen from West Point suggest all the natural beauty and variety of scene that made the valley so fertile a ground for artists' imaginings all through the 19th century.

settlement of the Hudson Valley had led as early as the 17th century to compromise and trade with the New Englanders to the north and east and the Quakers and Germans to the south in Pennsylvania. Without a theocracy like that of New England, which forbade any divergent religious sects, or like that of Quaker Pennsylvania, which frowned on military activities and the frolicking associated with resorts, the Hudson Valley was neither sanctified nor restricted. Benson Lossing expressed the notion of the valley as a tabula rasa, with its character open to definition in 1860:

> Unlike the rivers of the elder world, famous in the history of men, the Hudson presents no grey and crumbling monuments of the ruder civilizations of the past or even of the barbaric life so recently dwelling upon its borders. It can boast of no rude tower or mouldering wall, clustered with historical associations that have been gathering around them for centuries. It has no fine old castles, in glory or in ruins, with visions of romance pictured in their dim shadows; no splendid abbeys or cathedrals, in grandeur or decay, from which emanate an aura of religious memories. Nor can it boast of mansions or ancestral halls wherein a line of heroes have been born, or illustrious families have lived and died, generation after generation. Upon its banks not a vestige of feudal power may be seen because no citadel or great wrongs ever rested there. The dead Past has scarcely left a record upon its shores. It is full of the living PRESENT, illustrating by its general aspect the free thought and free action which are giving strength and solidity to the young and vigorous nation within whose bosom its bright waters flow.

In fact, in 1860 there were very significant historical associations with the Hudson for many Americans dating from Revolutionary War battles, and it was less than twenty years since the Rent Wars had removed the last vestiges of feudalism from landlord-tenant relations. However, Lossing was essentially right. From the earliest days, whoever had paid the lord of the manor his due was welcome to try and make a go of it in the Hudson Valley. Also, the central location of the valley in the colonies and its value as an artery of trade was established at the time of the Revolution and confirmed by the opening of the Erie Canal in 1825. Therefore, institutions typical of New York State and typical of the emerging character of the United States as a whole were planted in valley soil and flourished.

The Shakers

By the time these Shaker men and women were photographed at Watervliet in 1892, their society was in decline. The early strictures on photographs had been relaxed. In such formal portraits as this, the subjects wore deliberately archaic costumes, and the photographs were used as advertisements for Shaker seeds and herbs and storage boxes.

One of the first groups to come to the area for purposes other than trade or farming were the religious communards known as Shakers. The term "Shaker," a contraction of "Shaking Quaker," had been used to describe members of an 18th-century English sect who professed to be Quakers but were prone to leaping calisthenic dances when they worshiped. Under the leadership of "Mother" Ann Lee, nine Shakers arrived in New York, already the most liberal and cosmopolitan seaport in the colonies, in 1774. After a year of taking in washing to support her flock, Mother Ann led seven others upriver to Niskayuna, near Albany, in the manor of Rensselaerwyck where they settled on 200 acres in 1776. The society (renting land from the Van Rensselaer patroon for "8 Bush-

ells of wheat for every 100 acres'') grew apace and by 1787, under the official name of The United Society of Believers in Christ's Second Appearing, they had founded a second community at New Lebanon, in Columbia County near the Massachusetts border.

Ultimately, there were nineteen Shaker communities scattered from Maine to Kentucky; at their zenith 6,000 brothers and sisters lived in productive, celibate harmony in neat clapboard villages. The basic Shaker tenets had been established by Joseph Meachem, the successor to Mother Ann (who died in 1784), as confession of sins, celibacy, separation from ''the world'', and communal ownership of property. These were very specific, hardheaded points of doctrine, three of them at least dealing with actions as much as theology; and this literal grounding of the faith in well-cultivated acres may have accounted for the success of the Shaker way of life.

America generally was hospitable to religious groups of all persuasions in the 19th century, but the ones that lasted more than a few years and garnered more than a few members were the communes that drew on a working class farm population and

The serenity of Shaker life— some visitors found it enervating—is conveyed by the photograph of the members of the Watervliet community near Albany solemnly grouped around a bridge, beside their beehives.

looked toward very specific religious goals, such as the second coming of Christ. The Shakers, with their English working class background and membership of orphans and hired help, were disciplined to cherish the body as Christ's temple on earth and to preserve that temple, with hard work and temperate living, until Christ's imminent arrival. Preservation necessitated good farming and good business. Like the German communal societies such as the Rappites in Pennsylvania and the Amana Society in Iowa, the Shakers succeeded materially. High minded communal societies composed of philosophizing gentlemen, on the other hand, like Brook Farm near Boston, at which Nathaniel Hawthorne and philosopher Bronson Alcott lived, lasted only a few years.

When Benson Lossing visited the Shakers at New Lebanon in 1861, he found that 500 people owned and cultivated 10,000 acres of land. The Shakers lived in "families" of about 50 people, and, while tasks were strictly defined, the workers were assigned to each task on a rotating basis. "A place for everything and everything in its place" was one of their domestic watchwords, and, from pegs on the walls so that chairs could be hung up out of the way of dusting brooms to experimental rotation of crops, the Shakers found what seemed a divine routine for their lives. Rising at 4:30 AM, the brothers and sisters met at 6 AM in the dining halls where they ate rapidly and in silence, sitting at tables segregated according to the sexes. They then went to their tasks, reconvening for dinner at noon and supper at 6 PM. Jobs in the kitchen and dairy and at the loom for women and in the fields or in the manufacture of oval boxes, furniture, and clothing for men were rotated at intervals of six weeks, so that no one was bound by the monotony of a particular job, and all were proficient at every task. Because the Shakers saw themselves as mere custodians of their time (until the millennium should arrive) and their land, there was no hurry and, of course, no intra-familial competition. There was an atmosphere in a Shaker village of what journalist Charles Dudley Warner (who had discovered "Old Mountain Phelps" for the world) called a "freedom from excitement." The less well disposed called it lassitude. But it worked. Most Shakers lived into their eighties and nineties, long beyond the normal life span of "the world's people." It was only after the Civil War in a newly industrial America, when the cities offered regular wages and the lure of variety, that the Shakers had trouble recruiting converts who would pledge to remain celibate, and their numbers declined. At Watervliet (as the parent settlement near Albany came to be called) in 1875 there was a population of 56 males and 88 females, and 59 of these were over the age of 60.

The Resort Scene

U.S. HOTEL SARATOGA SPRINGS
74.

About 25 miles to the north of the serene Shaker village, Saratoga Springs offered physical, if not spiritual, rejuvenation in the early years of the 19th century. For the early Americans—particularly in the North—idleness was a sin, slightly less dangerous than some others only because it was passive. The theological doctrine that work and worldly success would be the natural evidence of a state of Grace coincided with the necessity for work in order to survive on the frontier. With any form of organized relaxation likely to be condemned, it was necessary for the first resorts to bill themselves as good for the health. There were several hot springs in the moun-

No less regimented than life at West Point, and as determinedly communal as Shaker living, the hotel life at Saratoga Springs moved according to schedules and standards set for every gesture. The United States Hotel, shown here around the turn of the century, shared the glory of summer days with the Grand Union and Congress Hall.

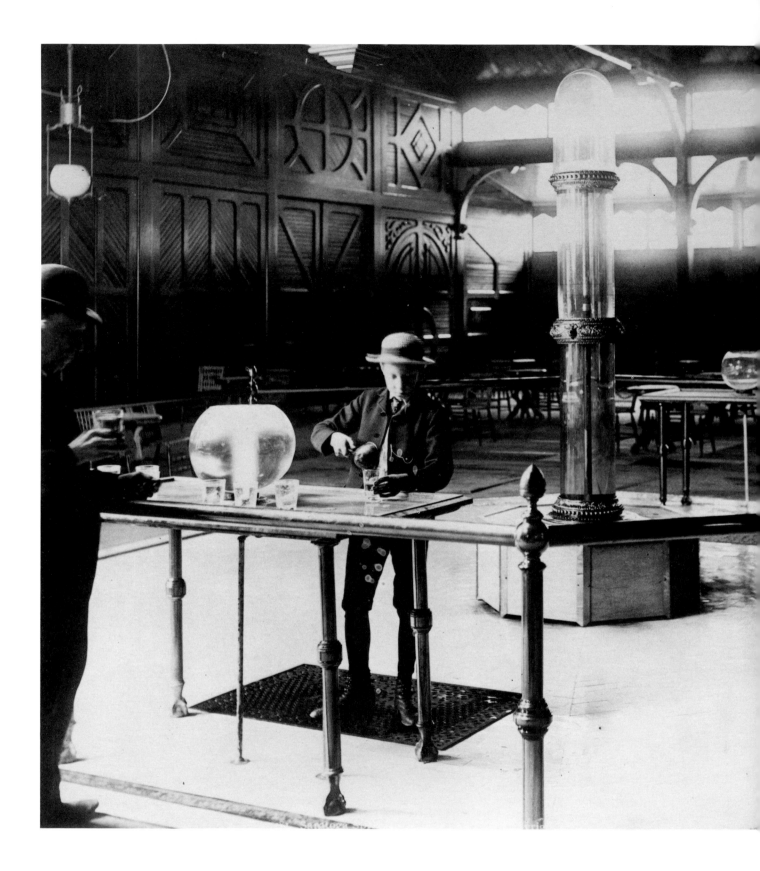

tains of the South where rich planters (always more amenable to diversion than Northerners anyway) had gone for several decades. Then Gideon Putnam put up the first hotel at Saratoga in 1800. The Hudson Valley's own literary eminence, Washington Irving, approvingly chronicled in later years how the "spa" had become popular: "It originally meant nothing more than a relief from pain and sickness; and the patient . . . called it a pleasure when he threw by his crutches and danced away from them with renovated spirits and limbs jocund with vigor." Irving bemoaned, however, the change that came to Saratoga with popularity. "Every lady . . . finding herself charged in a manner with the whole weight of her country's dignity and style, dresses and dashes, and sparkles, without mercy, at her competitors from every other part of the Union. . . ."

President Martin Van Buren made the spa his summer White House, and Saratoga did become the resort of political power and fashion, symbolized in the proud names of the Union Hall, Congress Hall, Pavilion and United States Hotels. Nonetheless it remained for some time a decorous and fairly quiet watering place with the principal entertainments being cards and an occasional dance ("hop") punctuated by enormous meals and regular doses of foul sulfurous water. English visitor James Silk Buckingham said in 1828 that guests at Saratoga ate "as if the world were coming to an end." Then, in 1864, some city magnates, bored by the absence of horse racing, which ceased when Southern guests removed their thoroughbreds at the outbreak of the hostilities, introduced racing on a professional scale. Between one season and the next, everything at Saratoga changed: "The Saratoga Association for the Improvement of the Breed of Horses" introduced not only fast horseflesh, but fast ladies and fast bets.

The mineral springs at Saratoga originally justified its existence as a resort. As descendants of the Puritans, Americans distrusted vacations unless they were strictly medicinal. The geyser of mineral water shot up within a glass dome in the pump house, left, for all to see while a young boy dispenses glasses for visitors.

One of the celebrations that was devised at Saratoga to fill the summer days was a Floral Fête. Carriages (above) and doll carriages (right) alike were decked with blossoms and paraded through the streets. The earnestness with which everyone regarded the affair was typical of the attitude of participants in resort and institution rituals.

Philip Hone, the New York City mayor and social figure whose diaries provide one of the most accurate and lively accounts of New York life between 1821 and 1851, described the old bustling but innocent Saratoga before the advent of the racetrack. In 1839, Hone saw "All the world . . . here, politicians and dandies; cabinet ministers and ministers of the Gospel; office holders and office seekers; humbuggers and humbugged; fortune hunters and hunters of woodcock; anxious mothers and lovely daughters; the ruddy cheek mantling with saucy health, and the flickering lamp almost extinguished beneath the rude breath of dissipation. . . ." After the Civil War, all of this changed. Men like "Boss" Tweed, the head of New York's political organization; "Commodore" Vanderbilt, who forged the New York Central Railroad; and President Ulysses S.

Grant, a leader of personal integrity surrounded by scoundrels, turned Saratoga into a resort where financial mergers and political bargains could be made away from the judgment of the legislature or the inquiries of stockholders. "Anxious mothers and lovely daughters" were replaced by "actresses" whose object was not marriage but money.

By the 1890's not only horse racing but gambling casinos cast a lurid gaslight aura in the north woods and very much cast the medicinal springs into the shade. "Big Jim" Morrissey, a former prize fighter, opened a casino—the Saratoga Club-House—on the snobbish criteria that no women or permanent residents of the town of Saratoga were to be allowed inside the premises. While the tycoons made deals and placed bets in the casino, their ladies, respectable and otherwise, sat on verandas nearly a mile in length or rode around town in high style. Lillian Russell, the actress whose 160 pounds were pressed into an hourglass figure that was the ideal of the period, reigned over Saratoga, riding in a carriage trimmed with silver given her by her friend "Diamond Jim" Brady.

At the height of its popularity in the 1890's, the Club-House kept $1 million in its safe, as large a sum as any of the casinos in Europe carried. The proprietor who followed Morrissey, "Dick" Canfield, Wall Street financier, art collector, and one-time proprietor of one of New York City's most famous gambling houses, spent $25,000 per year on the Saratoga Club-House grounds and kept a chef whom he paid $5,000 to work for a two-month season. Toward the turn of the century, however, the Astors, the Vanderbilts, and the Whitneys began to favor the race track so that Saratoga appealed again to New York's "400" Society rather than to the somewhat raffish big money men who preferred the Club-House. In 1907, Canfield closed the Club-House, which lay vacant for years. Although there were other gambling ventures at Saratoga, it remained a resort cultivated for its racing and justified by its waters.

Slightly more than 100 miles down the river, on a bluff in the Catskill Mountains, 2,200 feet above the river winding like a silver thread through the valley below, a hotel was built in 1823 that a practitioner of Victorian rhetoric later described as being "like a palace built for angels." The Catskill Mountain House, officially named the Pine Orchard House for the pine forests surrounding it, was a Greek Revival pillared hostelry that could accommodate 500 guests and, although not near any medicinal springs, was justified by its "sublime" view. The 19th-century Romantics were keenly alert to the morally elevating properties of Nature, taken in the right dosage, and the view from the Catskill Mountain House veranda seemed to be just the prescription. Harriet Martineau, the English travel writer, felt herself to be "humbled" by the "sublime" vista. During the 19th century, Thomas Cole, Asher Durand, and Frederic Church, artists of the Hudson River School, all painted the Mountain House, while Jenny Lind, President Grant, and President Arthur, among thousands of others, made the climb up the 12 miles from the village of Catskill in bumpy coaches (or, after President Arthur's visit in the 1880's, by railroad). In *The Pioneers*, James Fenimore Cooper has his woodsman hero, Natty Bumppo, answer when he is asked what one can see from the plateau where the Mountain House would later stand, "Creation! . . . all creation, lad! . . . The river was in sight for seventy miles under my feet, looking like a curled shaving, though it was eight long miles to its banks. . . ."

A Saratoga event that was sheer entertainment for everyone—except the performer—was the weekly ascent of Madame Carlotta. Known to the local press as "the intrepid lady," she rose (right) above Congress Park every Sunday from the summer of 1884 until the summer of 1889.

The theory of the sublime, whereby dramatic natural vistas were considered to be morally elevating, was almost as justifiable a reason for building a hotel as the presence of mineral springs. It was from such a perch as that of the Palisades Mountain View Hotel, that James Fenimore Cooper had his character Natty Bumppo assert that you could see "creation...all creation, lad!"

from Houghton's

Ideals and Ritual

Life at the resorts, whether attended for the elevation—moral and geographical—of the view or the pleasure of the waters, was ordered by schedules and rituals as fixed and unchanging as any routine of a Shaker village. One breakfasted, dined, and ate supper at fixed hours (perhaps only varied by "first" and "second" sittings); one promenaded at a certain hour; one took the waters and went to the casino, in Saratoga, at the fashionable time. There were appropriate clothes and probably appropriate small talk and expressions for the face at each ritual (guilt and apprehension at the gaming table, complacency and distaste at the mineral springs). The artificial groupings established by any society—whether for purposes of sanctity or pleasure—tell a great deal about that society. Any societal grouping beyond the essential farm family, farm village subsisting from its crops, or seacoast trading town was, to a degree, artificial in the early United States. The country had, according to Henry James, writing just after the turn of the 20th century, "no kings, no courts, no palaces, no . . . castles brooding over ancient wrongs . . ." to tell us how to behave and when. From church government initiated by the Puritans in New England in the 17th century to the "pursuit of happiness" guaranteed by the Declaration of Independence, American goals and institutions were created from scratch—and aimed at the ideal. The pursuit of these ideals created similarities between the Shakers withdrawing from the world at Watervliet and the vacationers withdrawing from seacoast cities to take the waters at Saratoga and the other Hudson River Valley institutions. They all shared one characteristic: almost everyone was there voluntarily and no one was there "naturally," in the sense that there was no economic base such as a farm or trading village to account for the community's founding. Beyond that, the Shakers and the sports at Saratoga shared, particularly in the early days of the communities, a high seriousness that is uniquely American. The Shakers had gathered together in expectation of the imminent end of the world, while the worldly vacationers felt that their gathering together had to be justified in terms of being beneficial to their health.

The first temperance society in America—that movement against the use of alcoholic beverages that resulted in Prohibition in 1920—was organized in 1808 in Saratoga County. And the first national president of the United States Temperance Union, organized in 1833, was a Van Rensselaer from Albany. How direct the

connection was between the Upper Hudson Valley's lead in the temperance movement and Saratoga's medicinal springs is not clear, but it suggests the climate of earnest moral concerns in which spa visitors and Shakers alike lived.

An amusing similarity between Saratoga and Watervliet, perhaps more attributable to personal taste than objective reporting, comes from James Silk Buckingham, the English writer. He praised lady guests at Saratoga for their beauty but commented, "They have no passion at all." Of the Shaker women he said, "The greater number were very plain . . . with an appearance of languor . . ." Plain or fancy, Buckingham found American women too serious, too earnest.

There is also a significant relationship between these societies and photography. Allowing for the long exposure time necessary to take a picture before George Eastman successfully marketed the Kodak in 1888, there nonetheless is a certain formality, if not rigidity, in the photographs taken at the various Hudson River Valley communities. The rows of spare Shaker dwellings imposed a pattern on the landscape less florid but no less directive than the

The close relationship between the formal public lives of people in such Hudson River Valley societies as resort hotels and West Point and the formality of composition in 19th century photography is evident in these images.

formal pathways making ornate circles around the pump-house pavilions at Saratoga. Photography historians have noted that early photographs performed an iconographic role; that is, a photograph of a family that had dressed in its best for the camera in the 1880's, for example, would suggest to a grandchild in 1915 that the family had been more prosperous than perhaps it was. With this ideal image in mind, the grandchild would then have a precedent, however contrived it had been, to live up to. With the photographs of the Shakers and the visitors to Saratoga, however, there is a union between the conditions of the subjects' lives when the photographs were taken and the formal demands of the photography of the period. The brothers and sisters at Watervliet were already on their best behavior for the Eye of God, not just for the eye of the camera, while the veranda of the Grand Union Hotel was filled with people who were certainly dressed in their best and engaged in a routine as rigid as any photographer's head clamp, holding a subject in place for the required exposure time. In the photographs of the formal, *public* lives at Watervliet and Saratoga, the medium of 19th-century photography—anything but "candid" as it was—and the nature of its subject were uniquely in accord.

West Point

An institution whose very nature was to impose order as the visible arm of government found a home in the Hudson Valley in the United States Military Academy at West Point. As early as 1783, General Washington, aware of both the necessity of a trained officer corps from his experience during the Revolution and the strategically central location of the Hudson, suggested that a military academy be established at West Point. On his last day of office in 1801, President John Adams appointed a faculty for a school for military gunners; in 1802 Congress enlarged the function of the school and officially named it the United States Military Academy.

Training to cope with the vast American continent as much as with enemy armies, these cadets of the 1880's extend a pontoon bridge out from the shore into the tranquil Hudson.

Members of the class of 1868 relax against a gas lamp along Professors Row at West Point. Since photography was still time consuming, even the most informal photographs required the subjects to hold their "candid" poses for a considerable time.

Ten cadets entered on July 4, 1802, to be trained as a "Corps of Artillerists and Engineers." Languishing through the early years of the Republic, West Point was revitalized in 1817 by the appointment of Major Sylvanus Thayer as superintendent. During his illustrious term (1817-33) the basic curriculum and system of discipline that he established made the academy's reputation strong enough to withstand recommendations that it be abolished. Again, with an earnestness of purpose toward national institutions that was possible because they were being built from the ground up (and very substantially built of Hudson Valley limestone at West Point), 19th-century Americans could debate the consistency of a training school for an elite professional officer corps with the ideal notion that the army should be a militia of free men defending their homes. The urge to fulfill "Manifest Destiny" by settling the continent, however, dictated that trained personnel lead armies against such opponents as the Mexicans. So, despite the undemocratic prevalence of rank at the military academy, "the Point" survived.

If the privilege of rank was to be conferred, however, so were the responsibilities; and West Point was determined to train officers and gentlemen. The duties, personal as well as military, of the cadets were typified by the classes of 1856 and 1857, both of which, because of an experimental five-year course initiated in 1856, were to graduate in 1861. Almost half of those graduates, 45 officers, were in the first Battle of Bull Run in July 1861. They fought on both the Confederate and Union sides, and many of them, including 2nd Lieutenant George Armstrong Custer, wrote and spoke affectionately and respectfully of their classmates in enemy ranks. In some cases they even had occasion to tend their former classmates in prison or on the battlefield.

West Point was observed in 1860 by the all-seeing Benson Lossing. A cluster of severe gray buildings perched on their point

As officers observe critically, cadets in summer whites move alertly through an artillery battery drill in 1894. The precision of West Point was matched across the river in the less congenial surroundings of Sing Sing Prison.

in the Highlands, the academy was magnificently situated on the river. At this time, West Point was the training field for about 300 cadets. The superintendent bore the rank of brevet colonel, and there were four companies of cadets, A, B, C, and D. The students had only one furlough in four years, from mid-June after their second year to a designated day in late August when they had to be back on the 2 PM boat at South Dock. There were, in the mid-19th century, no organized athletics—certainly no competitive intercollegiate ones—but the cadets did fence, ride, and dance in groups and couples. The "hops" (the same name for a supposedly informal dance that was used at Saratoga) only included lady partners when the river was not frozen. It was not until 1883 that there was a railroad on the west bank of the Hudson on which a lady could journey with the relative assurance that she would not be marooned scandalously longer than planned at her destination.

The strictness of West Point life was calculated to develop not only hard bodies, keen minds, unquestioning obedience, and, later in a cadet's term, the qualities of leadership, but by putting a whole class of cadets through the same hell weeks and hazing, an *esprit de corps* for their calling. Men who had gone supperless and stood sentry duty all night in a howling Hudson River snowstorm would have a closeness unknown to mere fraternity brothers in secular colleges. The camaraderie and esprit de corps were designed not only to encourage loyalty to the army but also to teach men regard for each other during the bleak tedium of life on the frontier posts where most of them served throughout the 19th century.

In the photographs of 19th-century West Point life there is the same correlation between the formality of life and the formality of the photographic style that was noticeable in photographs of Watervliet and Saratoga. A photograph taken in 1860 of cadets posing on the hand-pumped fire engine is an elaborate composition in symmetry and perspective. One cadet, perched on the central column of the engine, is also framed by the arch of a window in a wall behind him that slants away at just the angle to emphasize the horizontality of the engine itself. In fact, although definitely posed

The order and precision of life at West Point was underlined in a photograph taken in 1860 of cadets standing on one of the academy's fire engines in front of a series of arches. The fire engine is believed to be one of two purchased in 1839 with $1,900 appropriated by Congress for the purpose.

Cadets wheel through an artillery drill in 1879 on the plains of West Point, learning the intricate maneuvers that would protect them during service on the western frontier.

for the photographer, these cadets did live a life of drills and orderly formation, and, furthermore, operation of the fire engine itself required orderly coordination among the men pumping the water. The style of the medium perfectly fits the life it depicts.

Henry James, visiting his homeland for the first time in twenty years in 1904, wrote in *The American Scene* about the patterned nature of the image of West Point:

> I see it as a cluster of high promontories, of the last classic elegance, overhanging vast receding reaches of river, mountain-guarded and dim, which took their place in the geography of the ideal, in the long perspective of the poetry of association, rather than in those of the State of New York. It was as if the genius of the scene had said: 'No, you *shan't* have accent, because accent is, at the best, local and special, and might here by some perversity . . . interfere. I want you to have something unforgettable, and therefore you shall have type . . .

Sing Sing Prison

The regimentation of life at West Point was echoed at the prison, commonly known as Sing Sing, on the Hudson's East bank. As up to date in its way as West Point (it was the first prison in America to replace solitary confinement with theoretically rehabilitating labor), Sing Sing was also, however, unrelievedly brutal. The lock–step, here photographed sometime before 1900, was the only way the prisoners were allowed to move outside their cells.

Such efforts at rehabilitation at Sing Sing as a drawing class reflected the consistent American concern with self–improvement that influenced many of the valley's institutions.

The model of an arduous life, with enforced camaraderie, brought no esprit de corps whatsoever, it is likely, to the resident of another gray granite block contemporary with West Point on the east bank of the river. Sing Sing Prison was variously described as an enlightened resort of rehabilitation and, in a 1915 account, as belonging "to the dark ages—to the days of dungeons, thumbscrews, and cat-o'-nine tails . . . In Sing Sing there are two hundred cells into which in eighty years the sun has never penetrated . . ." In fact, to a degree, both views were true. With that tolerance for experimentation and concern for theory in the planning of institutions that characterized Hudson Valley life, Sing Sing was established in 1825 as an alternative to the dreadful Tombs Prison in New York City. Officially known as Mt. Pleasant State Penitentiary, Sing Sing took its familiar name from the neighboring village, which had adopted the Algonkian Indian name of Sint-sinck (meaning "stone on stone"). The village, in turn, changed its name to Ossining to avoid identification with the prison. Sing Sing represented a real advance in the penal system; it was one of the first prisons in which solitary confinement was replaced by a workhouse system in which the prisoners, theoretically, could rehabilitate themselves.

Benson Lossing enthusiastically asserted that at Sing Sing, "*Reformation* not merely *punishment* is the great aim, and the

history of the prison attests to the success of the effort." Well, yes and no. There was no doubt that having men working at manual labor was better for them physically than letting them lie in dungeons. However, the contract labor system meant that convicts were rented out to local businessmen and farmers for labor and their earnings, until 1886, went totally to the state, with the warden often getting a handsome rake-off. Sing Sing, located where it was partly because of the marble quarries nearby, furnished labor for quarrying the marble in New York's Grace Church and the Albany City Hall, among other Hudson Valley monuments. There was precious little rehabilitation involved, however, and the conditions of life in the prison, although perhaps better than the truly dungeon-like Tombs, were abominable. The stone cells that sweated water on the hottest July day were extremely small and lit only with slits set in the wall near the ceiling. The famous muckraking journalist Richard Harding Davis, writing in 1915, called

Richard Harding Davis, the popular early 20th century journalist, did an article in 1915 called "The New Sing Sing" in which he celebrated the reforms projected by the prison's new warden, Thomas Mott Osborne. The warden looking grim despite his jaunty cap posed in a cell block described by Davis as a place "into which in eighty years the sun has never penetrated...'

the buildings a "horror" and the prison "the most disgraceful exhibit in the state of New York." Prisoners were only allowed outside their cells when they moved in a body, walking with what was called "the lock step" in which each prisoner walked with his arms on the shoulders of the man in front of him. In 1900 prisoners were still locked in their cells from Saturday night to Monday morning in order to give the guards a day off.

Still, the prison had been innovative for its time and was contemporary with the first phase of Saratoga's popularity, the prosperity of the Shakers' greatest days, and the thin gray lines marching, wheeling, and drilling on the bluff at West Point. It was another of the new republic's social experiments (albeit less voluntary on the participants' part) that found a place in the Hudson River Valley.

The Vassar Heritage

From the prison's lock step to a college's daisy chains is a long way socially, but geographically the two were close in the 19th-century Hudson Valley. Poughkeepsie, home of the Hudson River chronicler Benson Lossing, was also the home of Vassar, one of the world's first women's colleges. When Matthew Vassar, a prominent Poughkeepsie brewer, funded the college that received its charter in 1861 and would adopt his name, it predated Smith College, Wellesley, and the first women's college at Oxford University, Lady Margaret Hall. The success of Vassar was followed by the establishment of numerous colleges and schools for young women in the valley, just as the presence of West Point inspired the founding along the river of military institutions for young men.

The story of Matthew Vassar and his school is typical of the combination of hard-headed business sense and enthusiastic idealism that flourished in the Hudson Valley. Matthew Vassar was born in England in 1792 and was brought to the Hudson Valley at the age of four. His uncle owned a farm in Dutchess County where he is said to have sowed the county's first acre of barley. In any case, when the ambitious Matthew was nineteen, he rebuilt a brewery of his father's that had burned. By 1842, Matthew was a successful brewer and the richest man in Poughkeepsie, as well as

president and chief promoter of the Hudson River Railroad. Boating interests on the river opposed the railroad, but Matthew saw correctly that it was essential for keeping the valley central as the lifeline of trade to the West. Aside from building his businesses in Poughkeepsie, Matthew took the waters at Saratoga, where he had his silhouette cut by a French artist; he served as president of the Poughkeepsie Lyceum of Literature, Science, and the Mechanic Arts (at which Ralph Waldo Emerson spoke); and he lent a receptive ear to an educator named Milo Jewett who wrote: " . . . if you will establish a real College for girls and endow it, you will build a monument for yourself more lasting than pyramids, you will perpetuate your name to the latest generations; it will be the pride and glory of Po'keepsie, an honor to the State and a blessing to the world."

The Observatory at Vassar was ruled by Maria Mitchell (in window at right), the astronomer who went to the college to teach in 1865, the year it opened, and remained for twenty–three years. Maria Mitchell's credo could almost be that of the school itself: "We must have a different kind of teaching...free thought and free inquiry are the very first steps in the path of science."

The touching and very gallant faith in culture as a tangible good, as attainable for the industrious as the riches of the earth and the river, was typical of the 19th-century American. Matthew Vassar ruminated on Milo Jewett's advice—and that of his favorite niece who herself ran a female seminary—and in 1861 Vassar Female College (soon changed by an act of the New York State legislature to simply Vassar College) was chartered. Matthew Vassar modestly noted that "It occurred to me, that woman, having received from her creator the same intellectual constitution as man, has the same right as man to intellectual culture and development."

Acting on this most modern theory, Vassar engaged James Renwick, Jr., the most prominent architect of his day, who designed Grace Church in New York and the Smithsonian Institution's "castle" administration building in Washington. Among the distinguished people on his first board of trustees were Samuel F. B. Morse, artist and inventor of the telegraph, and Benson Lossing, historian of the Hudson. In 1865, Vassar College opened its Gothic revival doors to its first 353 students. There were 30 faculty members, 22 of them women, including the famous astronomer Maria Mitchell. The tuition the year after the college opened rose from $350 to $400, with Matthew Vassar noting that the college president should *"Do all things Interlectural and Material the best,* and make *your prices* accordingly . . . I go for the *best* means, cost what they may and corresponding prices for tuition in return." Selling for the highest price the market would bear was good business sense, whether it was beer or culture.

Early on, Vassar was a voice for the perfectibility of humanity, specifically for women but essentially for both sexes. Although when Emerson lectured at Vassar, his topic was "The Man of the World" and he said insultingly that he thought ladies were incapable of "aiming their arrows at a star," President Eliot of Harvard in 1870 found Vassar women as well prepared as his own undergraduates in their various areas of study. It was not until 1914 that the administration finally gave permission for a formally organized Women's Suffrage Club, but in cultivation of the mind and implementation of diversions and conveniences Vassar was in the forefront. William James, the Harvard psychologist, lectured in 1896 on "The Psychology of Relaxation," but Vassar had already instituted field research on the subject in the form of lawn tennis, introduced in 1879, soon after it was brought to the United States from Bermuda.

The college had a traditional relationship with the river. In 1874 the college paper noted that the "junior class gave the seniors a moonlight excursion down the Hudson on the steamer *Mary Powell*," the most famous boat operating on the Hudson. It brought legislators to Albany, took cadets to West Point—and the body of George Armstrong Custer back to West Point after his last stand at the Little Big Horn—and carried excursionists for over sixty years. The custom of a junior/senior class excursion on the *Mary Powell* became a tradition until it was abandoned in 1885 because of what a Vassar chronicler records as "expense, danger from wandering ferry boats, and rather mysteriously detrimental remarks of newspapermen."

The odd detrimental remark to the contrary, however, the valley was proud of the college and its prestige, both socially and intellectually. Debates in the 1860's and 1870's about the worth of the education of women echoed earlier debates about the right of the Shakers to avoid swearing oaths and bearing arms. The debating in Congress in the 1840's about whether West Point should be abolished because it was "undemocratic" also helped thrash out the needs of the republic as they accorded with its ideals. The commercial abuse of prisoners' labor, originally started as a genuine reform movement when Sing Sing was built, stands as a warning in the examinations of the prison systems today. And the porches of Saratoga where the man of the world and his wife met and discussed propriety, fashion, the government, and the betting odds on the next race, all meant that in the Hudson Valley and its institutions the growth of the American nation was accomplished to a very real degree. Growing into some institutions, outgrowing others, the nation, in its youth and early adulthood, found education, justification, and pleasure in the valley's corridors and meeting places.

One of the lighter moments at Vassar occurred annually when the juniors treated the seniors to a boat ride (overleaf) on the beloved river steamer, the *Mary Powell*. Since the visiting of gentlemen callers was still strictly rationed in 1914, the juniors pinned up their hair, penciled on mustaches, and donned trousers to give the seniors beaux.

Excursion Steamers

The river steamers persevered despite competition from the railroads running along the river banks. The most popular during her nearly sixty years of service from 1861 until 1920 was the *Mary Powell* (top right). She made a round trip each day from Kingston to New York City under the captainship of one family, the Andersons. She carried Vassar girls to school for the first time, and she carried George Armstrong Custer back to West Point for burial after his defeat at the Little Big Horn.

A Hudson River sidewheeler in full steam could make about twenty miles an hour and was indeed a festive sight. Some time around the turn of the century the *Robert Fulton* (above), named after the man whose boat the *Clermont* had made the first successful steam run in 1807, puffed its way upriver, flags flying.

The river steamers had the joint character of commuter vessels and excursion boats. Sometime before 1904 one of the boats docked at Kingston (right) to load up with trippers who were heading down river for the day.

The old Dutch and English aristocracy in the Hudson Valley derived an authority from its ownership of land. The tranquility of two centuries of tenure was suggested when photographer Alice Austen recorded her mother and her mother's cousin, Mrs. Rusten Van Rensselaer, on the porch of the Van Rensselaer mansion at Fishkill on August 25, 1888 (right). The Van Rensselaers were the descendants of the only real patroons, as the putative recipients of vast 17th century Dutch land grants were to have been designated.

The Big Houses

The Big Houses

The tenant system in the Hudson River Valley, in existence since the colonial era, collapsed in the 1840's. Through this system—instituted by the Dutch and continued by the English—the large landowners rented farms to settlers and exacted archaic feudal payments of "four fat hens" or, more importantly, one quarter of the sale price if the farm was sold. There had been riots and less violent objections ever since the end of the American Revolution to a system that seemed to perpetuate the very Old World injustices that the Revolution had been fought to abolish. When tenants protested, however, they were told that the Van Rensselaers and Livingstons, to whom they were beholden, had been heroes of the Revolution and therefore could not represent anything un-American. This rather sophistic logic put off the day of anti-rent wars for a surprisingly long time. Finally, in 1846, after a series of belligerent attacks on rent-collecting sheriffs by farmers costumed in calico gowns and painted animal masks and carrying pitchforks, the state legislature passed a new constitution that abolished the system. The tenant system, in part at least, had kept the Hudson Valley relatively open, with farmers refusing to rent land there when they could settle on their own farther west. The look of the valley seemed bound to change after the manors were dissolved.

Coincidentally with the revolution in land ownership, however, came the flowering of the Industrial Revolution in America, and fortunes founded on ownership of land would be replaced by fortunes founded on trade, technology, and transportation. The low, rambling, stone and brick mansions in the Hudson Valley from which the Van Rensselaers, the Livingstons, the Schuylers, and the Philipses had ruled their kingdoms would be replaced by pretend castles, Moorish temples, and octagonal wonders to which captains of industry retreated after arduous days in their real kingdoms of city offices.

From the 1850's onward, the camera was one of a thousand mechanical contrivances, from the railroad to the telegraph, that changed life for ordinary people and enabled the new entrepreneurs to accumulate fortunes beyond earlier Americans' wildest dreams. One of the values of the camera is that it can magically transform light and the passing transitory scene into a permanent record, a pattern of history captured on a static sheet. Two pictures taken only a few years and a few miles apart in the valley symbolize the shift from the old wealth to the new. One is a photograph taken

from the ground level of a small boy wearing knickers and a cap in the style of the early 1900's standing ankle deep in the weed-filled lawn of an old house. The house is a Georgian structure, somewhat derelict, with a divided Dutch door standing open and the date 1713 hammered into the front of the building in iron numerals. The other photograph, also taken in the first decade of the century, shows the grandchildren of the financier Jay Gould sitting in miniature (but functional) French automobiles in the drive at Lyndhurst, the Gould estate on the Hudson.

The lone little boy, standing literally ankle deep in the land that had supported the now decrepit mansion near Albany over which the hush of eternity seems to have fallen, could symbolize the old aristocratic life along the river, while the little Goulds, sitting in their miraculous toy machines, could symbolize the new.

The houses built by the Dutch and English in the valley were simply designed and indigenous to the land their owners farmed and governed. They were the centers of working estates. That time had passed by the turn of the 20th century when this small boy was photographed standing in the weed filled lawn of the Glen Sanders mansion near Scotia, New York. The "1713" affixed to the front of the house places it in the days of the great valley manors.

Where the Schuylers and Van Rensselaers had gathered thousands of acres, the Goulds and Vanderbilts flung out thousands of miles of railroads, measuring more land than the early Van Rensselaers even knew existed. The 17th- and 18th-century river mansions were centers of communities; they were bases for land holdings farmed by tenants. They were, in a way, indigenous to the land. The later mansions were products of fortunes made elsewhere—beyond the valley—and from machines rather than land. These mansions were *ornaments* on the landscape, planted there for show; they were not as the older houses may be thought of, blooms on hardy native plants.

The tall brick houses and spreading trees of a street in Troy at the turn of the century convey the calm of the old, settled Hudson (right). Henry James wrote in *The American Scene*, on returning to the Hudson Valley after a trip West, that "one couldn't have felt more if one had passed into the presence of some seated, placid, rich–voiced gentlewoman after leaving that of an honest but boisterous hoyden."

The Original Manors

Life in the original manor houses along the river was ample and generous. The landowners modeled themselves on the English country gentry in their responsibility toward their tenants' welfare and their careful husbandry as well as their pretensions and lived in a high style that is customarily thought to have existed only on estates along the Southern rivers. In fact, Hudson River life resembled life in the South in several ways. For instance, New York was the last state north of the Mason-Dixon line to abolish slavery (1827). Harold Frederic, author of *In the Valley*, writes rather ex-

The Van Cortlandts received a manor from the English, a tract of land to be settled with tenants, in 1680. Eventually extending the holdings to 86,000 acres, the Van Cortlandts ruled from this mansion that, despite its touches of elegance, had the integrity of a sprawling farmhouse, built for use.

Frederick Philipse, the lord of Philipsburg Manor, which took in much of what is now Westchester County, built the Old Dutch Church in 1685; it looked much the same more than two hundred years later.

travagantly of manorial life: "No power of fancy can restore for you . . . the flashing glories of that spectacle: the broad, fine front of the Manor House, with all its windows blazing in welcome; the tall trees in front aglow with swinging lanterns and colored lights, hung cunningly in their shadowy branches after some Italian device; the stately carriages sweeping up the gravelled avenue. . . ."

At Clermont, a manor on the Hudson's east bank that eventually grew to 160,000 acres, granted to Scottish immigrant Robert Livingston, the inhabitants lived at the center of crucial affairs of the Revolution and early Republic. Clermont had been burned by the British in 1777 when the fight for control of the Hudson was at its fiercest. Robert Livingston, a descendant of the original Robert who helped draft the Declaration of Independence and served as chancellor of New York State, rebuilt the house at his mother's

urging. After serving as ambassador to France, he came home to his mansion opposite the Catskills and indulged his interests in scientific farming and such newborn mechanical marvels as the steam engine. It was as patron of Robert Fulton, who married Livingston's niece, that he saw the first successful steamboat, named *Clermont* in honor of the manor, work its way up the river in 1807. The Livingston holdings were divided and subdivided among heirs and connections but they remained vast, even after the loss of the tenant farms in 1846.

One of the big events in the lives of folk at quiet country houses such as the Van Rensselaers' was when the night blooming cereus made its once–in–a–decade appearance.

Clermont itself was echoed, although not duplicated, by a house called New Clermont, built a quarter mile away from the old one in the style of a French château. Old Clermont came to resemble the new house in the 1870's when a French château-style roof was added to the Georgian central block.

The Frenchifying of Clermont's clean Georgian lines (which reportedly was a Federal duplication of the colonial mansion burned by the British) was one example of the "modernizing" trend toward ornamentation and size of the various mansions that came to dominate the river. This grandiose approach had never been thought necessary when a house was simply the largest and most comfortable shelter a man could afford.

Alice Austen on another trip to the Van Rensselaer cousins at Fishkill photographed "Cousin Emily, Cousin Emmie and dog Beauty" at the foot of the piazza steps.

9453. „Sunnyside," Home of Washington Irving, Tarrytown, N. Y.

C.E.C. a. m.n

The mansions erected in the Hudson Valley in the 19th century, unlike the older houses, were built with money earned elsewhere. They were often fancifully designed to suggest English castles, or French châteaux, or even Moorish palaces. One of the first of the Hudson mansions to follow the owner's imagination in its design was Sunnyside, constructed by Washington Irving, the chronicler of the old Dutch way of life.

One of the most influential books ever written about American architecture and interior design, and a significant influence on later 19th-century Hudson Valley mansions, germinated in valley soil. Andrew Jackson Downing (1815-1852), the orphaned son of a nursery gardener, had been born at Newburgh and taken up as a protégé by the Austrian consul general, Baron de Liderer, who introduced him to many of the old river families. Downing, who was intelligent, handsome, talented, and insatiably ambitious, began to advise the people whom he visited on how to plant their lawns and gardens. Marriage to Caroline De Windt, of the De Windts of Fishkill, gave him the leisure to write *A Treatise on the Theory and Practice of Landscape Gardening Adapted to North America*. It was an immediate success upon its appearance in 1841 and was followed by a book on "rural cottages" and, in 1850, by *The Architecture of Country Houses*. Downing's popularity was increased after his tragic and romantic death when the Hudson steamship *Henry Clay*, on which he was traveling. caught fire from an overheated boiler during a race. After his death it was said of him, "the workman, the author, the artist were entirely subjugated in him to the gentleman."

Downing's influence, however, extends beyond architecture and gardening. In *The Architecture of Country Houses*, Downing

Irving's description of his house was of "a little, old fashioned stone mansion, all made up of gabled ends, and as full of angles and corners as an old cocked hat"—but in fact its charm was calculated and pure 19th century Romantic. The proprietor himself was photographed in his seventy—fourth year on the porch in 1856.

states that the first value of a home is that it is a civilizing influence on both the inhabitants and the neighborhood. This view, in 1849, was revolutionary in its quiet way. Before established communities and the labor-saving devices of the machine age were common in America, the primary value of a home, according to anyone's notion, rich or poor, would have been that it was *shelter*. A farmer setting up a homestead in the wilderness, whether he was a patroon with tenants at his command or a poor settler with his wife and children following their one horse on foot, would have cited protection—from the elements, natives, and animals—as the first reason for his house's existence. The community-oriented, display value of a home as a civilizing influence would have been an alien notion to practical settlers.

What allowed Downing to advocate choices beyond necessity, and what made them popular, was the increased prosperity that trade and machinery brought to mid-19th-century America, particularly the Hudson Valley. With reapers and combines to bring in the crops and steamboats and railroads to transport them, plus the new markets the railroads could reach, a leisured, moneyed middle class was being created that could consider the amenities of life. And some of the same machines that allowed time and money for

In *Hudson River Bracketed*, Edith Wharton, the novelist of New York Society mores, refers to Andrew Jackson Downing's classifications of architecture: "A. J. Downing, the American landscape architect, in his book on Landscape Gardening (published in 1842) divides the architectural styles into Grecian, Chinese, Gothic, the Tuscan, or Italian villa style and the Hudson River Bracketed." The Dinsmore mansion in Staatsburg, although Tuscan in outline and with a turret roof reminiscent of the Chinese, is, in sum, pure Hudson River Bracketed.

The increased monumentality of the Hudson River mansion as the 19th century progressed is evident in these views of the Averys' house at old Katonah (above), taken in the 1860's with its group of croquet players, and in the later Ardsley Towers (right), with its ebullient Queen Anne style architecture.

varied and elaborate houses also allowed the creation of jigsaw-cut trim, elaborate bargeboards, and interior paneling. Downing, with a newly-rich industrial aristocracy and middle class for readers, shunned the simplicity of the popular Greek Revival style, complaining that "without porches or appendages of any kind . . . the doubting spectator (could not know) whether the edifice is a chapel, a bank, a hospital, or the private dwelling of a man of wealth and opulence." Instead he suggested the Chinese, the Gothic, the Tuscan, or the Italian villa style. In satisfying his own taste he invented the Hudson River Bracketed, a board and batten cottage style, the peaked roofs of which were decorated with jigsaw trim and offered a compromise between Gothic aspiration and Italian solidarity.

Lyndhurst (right, top), built in 1840 and expanded in 1864-1865, when this photograph was taken, was a perfect example of Hudson River Gothic architecture. The grandchildren of financier Jay Gould, owner of Lyndhurst, posed in 1902 (right, bottom). Each child sits in his or her own French *voiturette* around the family Panhard-Levassor. When Helen Gould and friends were photographed in the sun parlor (above), Lyndhurst's Gothic edges had been softened by flowers and furbelows.

THE GOULD FAMILY AND ITS AUTOMOBILE STABLE

Downing, for all of his snobbishness (he divided dwellings into "cottages," "farmhouses," and "villas" according to the number of servants a family could afford to keep), was one of the first landscape architects to propose the idea of a suburb where people who neither lived off the land nor could afford to own estates would nonetheless benefit from more nature than a city garden could provide. For those who could not afford a suburban villa, he proposed public parks, the most famous of which, New York City's Central Park, was eventually implemented by Downing's protégé, Calvert Vaux. Downing was also instrumental in making fruit growing profitable in the Hudson Valley after the railroads and the Erie Canal shifted the center of wheat farming farther west.

Vanderbilts and Verplancks

Downing was a seminal as well as an attractive figure in the transition of the river valley from the agricultural principalities of the pioneer patroons to the truck farms and flower gardens of small farmers and industrial nouveaux riches. A contemporary but less attractive figure in the shifting landscape of the valley was Cornelius Vanderbilt, known as "Commodore Vanderbilt" (1794-1877), who had moved from running a ferry service between Manhattan Island and Staten Island to owning steamships (hence his purely "honorary" title) and eventually railroads. One of the most famous of the steamboat races (similar to the one in which Downing was killed in 1852) occurred in 1847 between George Law's *Oregon* and Commodore Vanderbilt's namesake ship, the *Cornelius Vanderbilt*, for a purse of $1,000. The Commodore lost that race, but it was one of the few contests he ever lost. He began to buy up railroads in the 1860's, seeing that they represented the future of transportation. In 1862 he gained control of the railroad that had snaked its way up the east bank of the Hudson to Albany in 1851 and within a few years combined it with twelve smaller lines between Albany and Buffalo to make the New York Central. When the Commodore died in 1877 (with his family standing around his deathbed singing "Come Ye Sinners, Poor and Needy"), he was the richest man in America, leaving a fortune of $100 million.

The next stage beyond the fanciful in Hudson River domestic architecture was the monumental (right). Frederick Vanderbilt's mansion at Hyde Park was completed in 1898 at a total cost of several million dollars. Designed in the Beaux Arts style by the architectural firm of McKim, Mead and White, which was more accustomed to working on the scale of New York's Pennsylvania Station, the Vanderbilt mansion seems only to maintain its status as a country house with the wicker chairs placed somewhat incongruously on the side porch.

The excesses of the 19th century extended to their voracious borrowing from the Renaissance, the oriental, the colonial, and the classical in the furnishings of their crowded interiors. The interior of Hilton's Woodlawn reflected most of these trends.

Not only were the new Hudson River mansions different in style and purpose, but the new gentry seemed to be different from the old. Judge Henry Hilton, posed (left) with his family before Woodlawn, on his 1,600 acre estate near Saratoga Springs. Hilton had been the lawyer for A. T. Stewart, the New York City dry goods king. After Stewart's death in 1876, Hilton issued an order barring Jews from the Grand Union Hotel at Saratoga, which the Stewart estate owned. New York's Jewish population in turn boycotted Stewart's store, which eventually went bankrupt. The judge nevertheless managed to die with a fortune of ten million dollars.

The agent of change employed by the Commodore in the valley was the railroad, bringing wheat and cattle from the West and facilitating communication between the rest of the nation and the country's canniest financiers in New York City. The story of what happened to one of the oldest river families, the Verplancks, when the railroad crossed their land depicts in miniature the conflict between the old landed fortunes and the new money of families such as the Vanderbilts. (For all his old Dutch name, the Commodore had come from a poor Staten Island family with only a Netherlandish ancestry in common with their rich river cousins.) The Verplancks had lived near Peekskill at Verplanck Point, just above the Tappan Zee, since early colonial times. The point borders about two and a half miles of green shoreline with a sandy beach. The Verplanck house was burned in 1776 by shot from the British warship *Vulture*. It was in the parlor of the Verplanck house that the Society of the Cincinnati—that hereditary order of Revolutionary War officers that Thomas Jefferson called "the root of pseudo-aristocracy"—was formed. A collateral descendant of the Verplancks, young Verplanck Colvin, would discover Lake Tear of the Clouds, the source of the Hudson, in 1869. The Verplancks sat proud and secure in their stone house with its Dutch gables and indignantly refused a real estate developer's offer of $250,000 for

When the Langdon House was originally built by the Delano family (to which Franklin Delano Roosevelt's mother belonged) in the 19th century, it was a stately house built in the Federal style. The Vanderbilt House (page 139), which replaced it on the site, was an inappropriately sumptuous palace.

Verplanck Point in 1835. Carl Carmer, in his anecdotal history, *The Hudson River*, tells what happened when the Hudson River Railroad decided to cross Verplanck Point:

> . . . thirteen years later (in 1848) when the Hudson River Railroad promoters offered them $5,000 for the right of way on which to run their noisy dirty engines the Verplancks turned them down so coldly and disinterestedly that the amazed financiers doubted the offer had been heard. Before the end of another year the property had been condemned at an appraised value of $1800 and the Verplancks forced to accept the decision. A new spirit had come to the banks of the Hudson, a spirit long evident on the water in the ruthless conflicts of the competing steamboat companies. The aristocrats were no match for the river pirates. Business was going to have its day on the Hudson. Verplanck was helpless before Vanderbilt.

The contrast in ways of life between the new aristocracy and the old could be seen almost literally next door to each other some miles north of Verplanck Point at Hyde Park. The estate took its name from Edward Hyde, Lord Cornbury, an 18th-century colonial governor who enjoyed dressing up in women's clothes, claiming that he was impersonating his royal cousin Queen Anne. Hyde

Park had largely been the property of the Bard family, one of whom was George Washington's military physician. The Bards sold a sizable chunk of land in 1827, and that piece was bought by John Jacob Astor in 1840. In 1895, in a gesture that might have served to suggest the handing on of the baton of social leadership, the Astors sold their Hyde Park holdings to Frederick Vanderbilt, a grandson of the Commodore. Frederick, the first Vanderbilt to go to college (Yale, '78), had increased his legacy of $10 million to a whopping fortune of more than $70 million. He kept $3 million in his checking account "just in case I want to buy something . . ." Having used his discretionary income to buy the land at Hyde Park, Frederick decided to go farther and build the most lavish mansion the Hudson had yet seen. McKim, Meade, and White, the prestigious New York architects who planned buildings on the scale of New York's Pennsylvania Railroad Station, designed the house, which cost $660,000 to build. Erected between 1896 and 1898 and costing $2 million to decorate, the house stands today in marble and stone, grandiosely embellished with such touches as a Baroque ceiling painting of nymphs and a satyr that the Vanderbilts had whitewashed over while they owned the house.

Monumental, impersonal, set somewhat incongruously in the landscape, having brought nothing to it and taking advantage of the landscaping and planting of previous owners, the Vanderbilt house stands aloof in contrast to the hospitable spread of its neighbor, Franklin Delano Roosevelt's home, known officially as "Springwood" but familiar to much of the world for more than a century as Hyde Park.

Kykuit, the mansion built by William Welles Bosworth for John D. Rockefeller in 1913 at Pocantico Hills, is typical of the grand Beaux Arts style of the Hudson River mansions of the late 19th and early 20th centuries.

The Roosevelts

The Roosevelts were an old Dutch river family (Nicholas Roosevelt had been a partner of Chancellor Livingston and Robert Fulton in developing the *Clermont* in 1807), and FDR's great-grandfather, a city merchant and state assemblyman, had bought property at Hyde Park in 1819. Springwood itself, however, had only been in the Roosevelt family since 1867 when James Roosevelt, FDR's father, bought a clapboard-covered brick farmhouse built in 1826. James turned the house into a good example of Hudson River Bracketed with a square turret, an encircling porch, and a decorated bargeboard under the roof. He took his bride, the former Sara Delano, there in 1880, and she commenced making the house over into a rambling Georgian stucco structure with fieldstone wings.

As Franklin's family grew, along with his political prominence, the wings of the house also expanded (although the central structure was essentially complete by 1916). At its fullest extent it resembled in its sprawling essential relationship—to the entire nation this time—the old indigenous Dutch manor houses and their governmental relationship to the land. This relationship between the house and the land was recognized in a 1917 discussion between Franklin, then Assistant Secretary of the Navy, and Eleanor on one side and Franklin's strong-willed mother, Sara Delano Roosevelt, on the other. Both sides acknowledged the relationship, but when Sara expressed the hope that the house would always be a family seat, she was met by opposition from Franklin and Eleanor, who said that it should eventually be turned over to the public for a park.

The Roosevelts and the other prominent families along the lower Hudson made the river a recreational extension of their shoreline estates in both summer and winter. Preparing for a winter ice yacht regatta in the 1880's, James A. Roosevelt *(center background)* stands casually while the young Miss E. C. Roosevelt approaches the yacht "Avalanche" in her pony sleigh.

Getty Square Yonkers 1876
Presented to George Mullin
Proprietor Getty House by John Sutherland 1916

The Octagon House

The function of the mansion as a decorative statement led to some extravagances and follies in the constructions of the later 19th century. Andrew Jackson Downing's benediction on neo-Gothic castles "where the neighboring mountains or wild passes are sufficiently near to give that character to the landscape" promoted wooden castles and ruins constructed from scratch, as well as imitation castles that were supposed to bring out the resemblance of the Hudson to the Rhine.

Then there was the house built just north of Fishkill according to the ideas of phrenologist Orson Fowler. Fowler invented the octagon house. The author of *A Home For All, or the Gravel Wall and Octagon Mode of Building*, published in 1849, Fowler combined wishful thinking with sound design concepts that were nearly a century ahead of his time. Fowler was a classmate of the future clergyman Henry Ward Beecher at Amherst College and had accompanied Beecher to Boston while they were still in college. There they heard a discourse on the "science" of phrenology— telling people's characters by feeling the shapes of their heads. Fowler was a convert to the idea, his conversion perhaps helped by the fact that he promptly returned to college and made 2¢ a head revealing his classmates' characters to themselves. Setting up a studio in New York City, lecturing around the nation, and writing *Phrenology, Proved, Illustrated and Applied*, Fowler made a fortune. Influenced by his desire for publicity and his inherent flamboyance, he hit on the idea of the octagon when he decided to build his dream house. Perhaps reminded of the thousands of heads he had felt, Fowler declared that the sphere was the most beautiful shape in Nature. It incorporated, he declared, the most space in the least material. Because he thought it was impractical to build a spherical house, however (even Fowler was not advanced enough to work out the 20th-century's geodesic dome), an octagon would employ the sphere's advantages. There would be more exposure to sunlight in the inner rooms, there would be no waste corners, and the house could be partially heated by a central glass dome radiating over the point where the curved octagonal sections of the roof met. Fowler's own house, finally opened in 1858 to great interest after ten years in the building, was "befouled," literally, when the porous walls of the cesspool allowed seepage into the well, and several house guests died of typhoid.

Nevertheless, the octagon had flourished widely as a fad between approximately 1850 and 1853. Fowler strove for one design that would be practical and aesthetic and that would exemplify what is only now coming to be appreciated as essential conservation of energy in heating and lighting. Examples of the octagon dotted not only the Hudson Valley but the landscape of the entire nation from New England to the Mississippi River.

Frederick Church and Olana

The Luminist painter Frederic Edwin Church was visionary in a completely different way from Fowler—and far less practical, despite Fowler's somewhat uncritical acceptance of incompatible ideas. Church built a Moorish fantasy, Olana, across the Hudson from the village of Catskill in 1870. If Fowler's visions were of science translated into geometry, Church's were of the intensely colored landscape of the imagination. Church was a disciple of Thomas Cole, one of the best-known painters of the Hudson River School of landscape artists. When Cole died in 1848, Church carried the banner of the Hudson River School's grand romantic landscapes several steps further. Using the synthetic pigments available in the 1850's to paint the hot reds and yellows of tropical sunsets and volcanoes, Church and other Luminists dealt with distance and light in their paintings in a way that presaged the Impressionists' breaking up of color into light in the art of the 1870's and, socially, reflected the confidence of a pre-Civil War America in the riches of its seemingly infinite land. Although Church's huge landscapes went out of fashion in the 1880's—one critic dismissed his vibrant *Morning in the Tropics* (1877) as a "magnificent drop curtain"—his untrammeled Romanticism had reflected a national mood and led him farther artistically than either his peers or successors suspected. His *Heart of the Andes* was sold in 1859 for $10,000, which was then the highest price ever paid for a painting by a living American. His resurgent popularity is demonstrated by the fact that in 1979 his painting *Icebergs* (1861) brought $2.5 million at auction, which was the highest price ever paid for a painting by an American to that date.

Olana received more of Church's creative attention after his hands were crippled by inflammatory rheumatism in the 1880's, and he had virtually ceased to paint. The house is an exotic confection of yellow rough-cut stone, embellished by polychrome brick, glazed Persian and Mexican tiles, and wooden decoration. Moorish arches confront the Catskills across a magnificent vista of fertile plains bisected by the river. Besides the arches, there are a turret crowned by a roof decorated with colored slates in a design that looks like a Persian rug, a gallery with Persian pillars, and a kiosk-like studio added to the building between 1888 and 1891. Church was ecstatic about his creation. "I can say," he claimed, "as the good woman did about her mock turtle soup, 'I made it out of my own head.'" In fact, he had worked on the plans with Calvert Vaux, Andrew Jackson Downing's colleague.

A mansion that aspired to the heights of Hudson River Valley exotica was Olana, the Moorish seat of Frederic Church, a famous 19th century landscape painter. Begun in 1870 its style was described by Mrs. Church as "Persian adopted to the Occident."

Charles Dudley Warner, the journalist whose 1878 *Atlantic Monthly* article defined the Adirondack guide as a genuine tourist attraction, was photographed in the Court—or central—Hall of Olana in 1886.

Young visitors stand on the front steps of Olana in 1889. The Moorish arch of the doorway and its border of blue tiles made the entrance reminiscent of a Persian mosque or city gate (left).

Church's yearning for a medium equivalent to his intense aesthetic feelings produced Olana. It is almost as though the experimentation of his work with synthetic paints and the grandeur of scale he used in his canvases never quite met his private vision. Olana, if not the completely satisfactory expression of Church's views—he tinkered with it, building and changing until he died—may have come as close as any of his work on canvas. In his work on country houses Andrew Jackson Downing had written that the owners of villas should be "men whose aspirations never leave them at rest—men whose ambitions and energy will give them no peace within the bounds of rationality." To the degree that Olana is a delightful excursion outside the bounds of rationality, Frederic Church was Downing's perfect villa owner.

Moving along the river and in time, one proceeds from the low stone and pure Georgian mansions of the old Dutch families to the personal statements of wealth and taste—good, bad, and varied—of the later 19th century. The river, whether as trade route or as artistic setting, was the reason for the settlements and the houses. Of all the world, only in America, and of all America, only along the Hudson, are a Dutch farmhouse, a Georgian manor house, a French château, a castellated ruin, and a Moorish temple strung side by side, each not only representing the era of its building, but also suggesting other worlds of the imagination.

Bridges

The Hudson River was, for 250 years, a very important means of transportation. As the technology of the 19th century diversified transportation, however, the river became as much a barrier as an avenue. Bridges, which had spanned the narrow upper river from the late 18th century, were projected for the broad lower reaches. The Harlem River, joining the East and the Hudson Rivers at Manhattan's north end, is narrow and was bridged in the 17th century, but the first major edifice across the Harlem River was, ironically, a bridge for water. In 1842, New York City built an aqueduct and reservoir system to tap the Croton River, a tributary of the Hudson. When it was built, the High Bridge was compared to Europe's Roman aqueducts and called America's proudest structure.

Bridges crossed the rivers of pedestrians and carriages flowing along city streets, as well as crossing the rivers around the city. The "Bridge of Sighs," modeled on the famous Venetian Bridge, served a similar purpose, crossing between courthouse and prison (above).

The Williamsburg Bridge, opened in 1905, just north of the Brooklyn Bridge, supplanted the Brooklyn Bridge as the longest suspension bridge in the world. It was thought of as a symbol of consolidated New York and was hailed as "the highest achievement of the utilitarian" by the *Brooklyn Daily Times*.

The first modern bridge across the Harlem River was the Washington Bridge, built in 1889, which consists of two spans and which was designed for the carriage traffic that the High Bridge was too narrow to handle.

When the "New East River Bridge," soon to be known as the Williamsburg Bridge, was built in 1905, it was hailed as a triumph of contemporary engineering (right).

The City and the Harbor

The City and the Harbor

The Civil War was the great divide, not only in terms of how America looked at itself constitutionally and socially, but also in economic terms. Before the Civil War, the United States was primarily a small agricultural nation. After the Civil War, industry accelerated and ultimately became more important than agriculture. The proportion of urban residents continued to increase until there were more city dwellers than rural inhabitants. It was after the Civil War, therefore, that New York City, despite earlier prominence, came into its own as an international center of commerce. Steamships with metal hulls took over the international trade from wooden ships, the railroad took over internal transport from the river boats, the first skyscrapers appeared between 1868 and 1883, and the city began to assume both the character and appearance that it now has.

The mid-19th-century change in character—for the entire United States and the Western world as well as New York City—involved the matching of a burgeoning technology with resources required to feed the engines, mills, and wheels of the new era. New York City, poised at the mouth of the Hudson River, one of the East Coast's most significant internal trade routes, also boasted one of the finest natural harbors in the world. Like the nation it would come to lead in commerce and culture, New York had a wealth of natural advantages. When the railroad and the steamship met chronologically in the middle 19th century, it was natural that the narrow island of Manhattan would be the junction.

From its founding, the salient fact about New York City has been the location of Manhattan Island in the harbor. It is the city's placement at the meeting of the river and the sea that is the source of its power. Traditionally, cities have grown up on rivers, the easiest transportation routes, but the combination of a great natural harbor with a river that has a channel 150 miles into the interior deep enough for oceangoing vessels gave New York an advantage that no other North American city could match.

Demonstrating the unique importance of the conjunction of river and ocean in New York harbor, vessels in 1895 docked beside railroad loading piers. The advent of ocean-going steamships in the 1850's had made the west side of Manhattan as desirable a docking area as the east. Sailing ships had been able to move directly out of the East River, which never froze, while the broader Hudson was an advantage for steamships. In 1892 (overleaf) sailing vessels still dock in the East River, and local urchins enjoy cooling off.

New York & Lake Champlain Transportation Co.

THE
IRON
LINE

The harbor, with its islands, provides 650 miles of shoreline and was described in 1524 by Giovanni da Verrazano, the Florentine explorer who was probably the first European to see it, as "a most beautiful lake three leagues in circuit." Robert Juet, an officer on Henry Hudson's *Half Moon*, described the harbor as "a very good land to fall in with a pleasant land to see" in 1609. These were probably the last references to New York harbor that left out human activity. Practical and tolerant, the Dutch and their English successors encouraged a polyglot population of Huguenots, Germans, and Walloons, who busily traded along the coast and with England. Boston and Philadelphia also had good harbors and energetic traders, however, and it was not until after the Revolutionary War that New York really became the commercial and industrial leader among American cities.

The beginnings of a transportation network focused on New York coincided with regularly scheduled international shipping, and both contributed to New York's growth. The Erie Canal, begun in 1817 and completed in 1825, brought the Western grain trade (grain being a traditional New York City export from the time of the Dutch) straight across to Albany and down the Hudson. In 1818 the Black Ball Line started running the first scheduled freight and passenger vessels, so that merchants could count on shipping cargo from New York on certain dates, instead of having to wait for a vessel to be filled before it sailed. The easy arrival of goods in New York via canal and river and dependable outbound shipping made New York the most convenient port for the entire import/export trade of the United States.

The same scheduled shipping that channeled trade to New York also channeled the growing number of European immigrants through the port. Until the 1880's, each individual state was responsible for its own immigrants and New York, eager to increase its labor force—initially for working on the Erie Canal—implemented a series of public works programs that welcomed immigrants. Many new arrivals, at least for a transition period, based themselves in the city and contributed to the population growth. Others settled permanently, found jobs, and sent for family members, thereby cementing the city's multinational character.

Finally, when Andrew Jackson outlawed the Bank of the United States as a monopoly (contributing to the Panic of 1837), the Philadelphia financial community collapsed, allowing an already prosperous Wall Street to take the lead. New York, which had a population of 100,000 in 1815, grew to 300,000 in 1840 and 515,550 in 1850. From 1820, New York was the most populous city in the country.

Development of the Port

When there were thirty-five ferry lines in the harbor the city's Department of Docks and Ferries had many buildings around lower Manhattan and Brooklyn, including these two. South Ferry (above) is shown in half of a stereoscope view. The building on the right was decorated in bunting, the era's festive expression at any holiday.

New York's appearance reflected its growth and prosperity. An English visitor in 1846 wrote: "the port of New York exhibits itself in its most imposing aspects . . . being covered as far as the eye can reach, with a forest of masts and rigging, as dense and tangled in appearance as a cedar swamp." The island of Manhattan was built up as far north as 14th Street in 1850, and piers surrounded the streets of red brick row houses that were punctuated by church steeples that seemed themselves a landlocked version of the ships' masts. In 1853 there were one hundred twelve piers, fifty-five on the Hudson (called the North River by New York seamen since the days of the Dutch, who called the Delaware the South River), and fifty-seven on the East River. The shipping activity on the Hudson side of Manhattan was a recent development in the 1850's. As described in Robert G. Albion's *The Rise of New York Port*, a count of the ships docked on a day in 1836 showed that "of the square-rigged ships and brigs, the aristocrats of the sea lanes, 305 were moored in East River and only 39 in North River."

The Staten Island Ferry, photographed plowing through the harbor by Staten Islander Alice Austen sometime between 1890 and 1900, was one of nearly three dozen different ferry lines plying the harbor in those days. Today there is only the Staten Island line left.

The advent of oceangoing steamships allowed the Hudson to become a vital part of New York City's harbor industries. Samuel Cunard, a Halifax, Nova Scotia, shipowner and founder of the great Cunard Line of steamships, established the North American Royal Mail service route from Liverpool to New York in 1847. With Cunard regularly running ships, the United States Post Office asked for bids for an Atlantic mail service under the American flag, and a New York shipper, E. K. Collins, started the rival Collins Lines in 1850. Before the development of the oceangoing steamship, the Hudson had been impractical for docking ocean vessels, because the winds were such that while ships could sail directly out of the East River into the bay, they had to be towed out of the Hudson, and while the East River was almost entirely salt water and therefore did not freeze, the Hudson not only froze frequently during the winter but also carried crushing ice floes from upstream. The steamships, however, were impervious to wind, relatively impervious to ice, and needed the broader Hudson in which to turn. So,

When the Brooklyn Bridge was completed in 1883, it had been fourteen years in the building and more than twenty–five in the planning. Designed and executed by John Roebling and his son Washington Roebling, the bridge was not only the greatest engineering feat the world had ever seen, but one of the world's great architectural statements. Within two decades the East River would be crossed and recrossed by other bridges, forever outmoding the ferries that had operated there for more than two hundred years.

Singer Tower and Hudson River. C12169

Copyright 1917 by Irving Underhill N.Y.C.

In these two photographs, taken no more than twenty years apart, the old South Street docks (above) are still a forest of masts around the turn of the century. The new Singer Tower, photographed in 1917 (left), overlooks Hudson River docks for steamships, but even the modern technology that built the vessels and the tower could not keep up with progress: from 1898 to 1913 the commerce coming into the port of New York more than doubled while wharf space did not increase.

Seeing lower Manhattan much as it appeared during this World War I naval celebration, Henry James had written: "nature and science . . . joyously romping together, might have been taking on again, for their symbol, some collective presence of great circling and plunging, hovering and perching seabirds, white–winged images of the spirit, of the restless freedom of the Bay . . . "

after Samuel Cunard built a terminal at Jersey City, the Hudson developed as bustling a dock life as the East River. The Collins Line went bankrupt in 1858 after several disastrous ship losses and the expenses incurred by trying to beat Cunard's record for speed, but the Hudson was established as an active part of the harbor.

While the large ships carrying trade to and from New York crowded the piers, the number of craft carrying passengers and freight among the harbor islands, toward Long Island Sound, and up and down the Hudson, increased with the population. The ferry line that was the foundation of the Vanderbilt fortune was only one of fifteen in the harbor. New York Harbor is unique in the number of islands that dot its huge expanse of water. Because of these, there was always a busy intra-harbor traffic. The first ferry was established in 1638 between Brooklyn and Manhattan and had to be summoned by blowing horns that were hung on trees near the ferry slips on either side. Robert Fulton, builder of the world's first functional steam-powered vessel, developed a double-hulled steam ferry in 1814. It had an identical bow and stern, so that the ferry could come and go on its route without turning around—a characteristic retained by all New York harbor ferries, down to today's sole survivors, the handful of passenger boats on the Staten Island Ferry line.

By the early 1900's, there were thirty-five ferry lines, one of which included the massive train-ferry boat, the *Maryland*. It carried the Pullman cars on the Pennsylvania Railroad coming up from Philadelphia and Washington, around the foot of Manhattan to the Connecticut shore and returned with cars coming from Boston. Henry James took the *Maryland* in 1905 and wrote in *The American Scene:* "the easy and agreeable attainment [of his aim to proceed to Boston without leaving his Pullman car] was to embark on one of the mightiest (as appeared to me) of trainbearing barges and, descending the western waters, pass round the bottom of the city and remount the other current to Harlem; all without 'losing touch' of the Pullman that had brought me from Washington . . . The Bay had always, on other opportunities, seemed to blow its immense character straight into one's face—coming 'at' you, so to speak, bearing down on you, with the full force of a thousand prows of steamers seen exactly on the line of their longitudinal axis; but I had never before been so conscious of its boundless cool assurance or seemed to see its genius so grandly at play. This was presumably indeed because I have never before enjoyed the remarkable adventure of taking in so much of the vast bristling promontory from the water, of ascending the East River, in especial, to its upper diminishing expanses."

The "vast bristling promontory" that lower Manhattan presented to James is a familiar image today in thinking of New York. It is this monumentality of image—the picture of the city as crowded with skyscrapers, triumphal arches, and people; the picture of the river as tunneled under, bridged over, and channeled by shipping—that comes down to us traditionally. The photographs of the lower river seem modern, even when the people on the sidewalks wear period clothes or there are horse-drawn vehicles on the avenues, in a way that photographic scenes farther up the river do not.

Fifth Avenue, on the occasion of its famous Easter Parade around the turn of the century seemed to be the core of the "vast bristling promontory" that Henry James saw from the harbor. More private fortunes were represented in the Fifth Avenue mansions than in any other street on earth.

173

When the Flatiron Building —so–called because of its resemblance to an iron of the period—was erected in 1902 at the corner of Fifth Avenue and Broadway, it was confidently expected by skeptics that it would tumble in the first high wind.

Grace Church, built at the corner of Broadway and 10th Street in 1847 and designed by architect James Renwick, was evidence of the popularity of the Gothic mode in town as well as in country mansions such as Lyndhurst. Grace Church was the place of worship of Astors and Rhinelanders—the city's finest families—and its sexton was known to be an unofficial arbiter of society.

In its attempt to live up to being the nation's first city, New York began to erect monumental architecture and commemorative structures over the old red brick residences. The Washington Square Arch at the foot of Fifth Avenue boldly proclaimed America's imperial age (above).

Yearning for the endorsement of true aristocracy, holders of New York fortunes such as the Vanderbilts sought alliances through marriage with European nobility. At the wedding of Consuelo Vanderbilt and the Duke of Marlborough in 1895 at St. Thomas's Church (right, both), tophatted and befurred guests milled about before the ceremony, and footmen lined up.

City Photographers

The teeming multitudes of the city were, of course, made up of individuals, and Alice Austen attempted to photograph various economic groups. A street cleaner pauses on June 17, 1895.

The photographers of turn of the century New York seem to have been sharply defined in their choice of subject. Many were professionals, such as the Byrons, father and son, who photographed New York society for more than sixty-five years, and some were dedicated reformers, such as Jacob Riis, whose shots of the city's slums helped to pass protective legislation for new immigrants

dwelling on the Lower East Side. For the most part, whatever their motivation for taking photographs, the points of view are as assertive as the leading edge of the new Flatiron Building, thrusting uptown from the junction of Fifth Avenue and Broadway toward New York's future.

One exception, one photographer whose eye seems to have been as eclectic in terms of subject as her technique was sharp, was Alice Austen, a woman from Staten Island who was suited by her residence and background to take a slightly distanced stance from the city. Alice Austen (1866-1952) was what used to be called a maiden lady of gentle birth. She was born into modest wealth and comfort, the descendant of a family that had lived on Staten Island since before the Revolutionary War. One of the prized Austen possessions was a section of the monstrous chain that an ancestor

The golden dreams of New World wealth have never been fulfilled for everyone, and at the base of taller and taller skyscrapers was the poverty of such people as this organ grinder, who found a home on the city streets.

Known today for its fish, the Fulton Market around the turn of the century was a depot for all sorts of foodstuffs coming into Manhattan from Long Island and upriver farms. Here the workers at a chicken and turkey market stare at the camera.

had forged for George Washington's army to pull across the Hudson at West Point, thus keeping the British fleet from sailing up the river. Alice Austen's roots in the life of the old, pre-industrial Hudson Valley (she had Van Rennselaer cousins who lived at Fishkill) gave her an interest in river and harbor life, as well as the busier life of the city. In an objective style she photographed the new skyscrapers and newly-arrived immigrants as "types"—types of buildings and types of people, representative of a school of architecture or a level of society. This was very different from the formal but warm group photographs she took of family and friends. Her photographs of city life allow us to see in its component elements the beginning of modern, urban life at the mouth of the Hudson River. Alice Austen was a meticulous craftsman. Her pho-

NEW WOMAN – RIVERSIDE DRIVE.

tographs are usually labeled as to the exact date, time of day, the weather, the light, and the exposure time she used. Her precision could almost be seen to reflect the clockwork integration of the individuals she photographed into the vast mechanism of the city itself.

Past Alice Austen's vantage point at her home on the Narrows, the channel between Staten Island and Long Island that leads into the harbor, sailed the ships from Hamburg and Rotterdam that sometimes brought as many as a million immigrants a year to the Port of New York between 1870 and 1914.

Always hospitable to the new and daring, the city offered relatively level streets for the "New Woman" of the 1890's who donned bloomers and set forth on her bicycle.

Processing Immigrants

260. IMMIGRANT LANDING STATION, N.Y. COPYRIGHT 19

Ellis Island, opened in 1892 as the center for immigration, processed an average of 3,000 immigrants a day in the years before World War I.

From the early 19th century the port of New York was one of the principal centers of immigration in the nation. In 1855 Castle Garden (overleaf) on the Battery was leased as a center for processing immigrants. Once landed at Ellis Island (overleaf, right), immigrants had to pass literacy and health examinations or be turned back to their point of debarkation.

New York had been the favorite point of debarkation for immigrants since the 1820's, when the packet boats offered quick transportation up the Hudson and digging the Erie Canal offered work for the new arrivals. Well before the Civil War, the influx of immigrants was sufficiently large that the New York State Immigration Commission was established. The commission leased old Castle Garden, the round bastion-like structure on the Battery that had been a public reception hall when the Marquis de Lafayette visited in 1824 and a theater when Jenny Lind, "the Swedish Nightingale," had sung in the early 1850's, and turned it into a center for processing immigrants in 1855.

In 1865, *Harper's Weekly* reported that Castle Garden "has afforded a haven of security for immigrants . . . Besides having a place of safety for the landing of his effects, the emigrant (sic) is relieved from the exploitation of runners and of the sellers of bogus railway tickets." By 1882 the federal government had begun to take over the administration of the immigration bureau from the state, and in 1892 the immigration office opened the processing center on Ellis Island in New York Harbor. Once known as Gibbet Island from the hanging of a pirate in the 18th century, Ellis Island processed an average of three thousand immigrants a day in the years before World War I. Ellis Island was closed as a center of immigration in 1954.

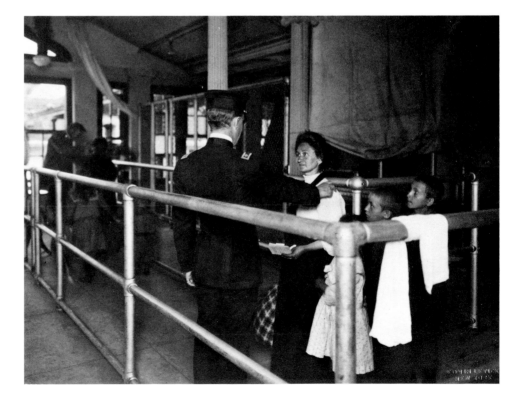

Having endured the rigors of the sea voyage and the examinations of Ellis Island, these immigrants sit with their luggage at the Battery (above), seemingly stunned about where to go next.

Although it was only third class passengers who had to pass through Ellis Island, a single ship such as the *Westernland* of the Red Star Line carried as many as 2,000 steerage passengers on each trip. A one way ticket cost approximately $20.

The Statue of Liberty

The best-known immigrant to New York Harbor, the Statue of Liberty, officially known as Liberty Enlightening the World, was often an immigrant's first glimpse of the New World. The statue is made of hammered copper sheets, sculpted by Frédéric Auguste Bartholdi, a French artist known for his monumental works. The sheets were welded to a framework of iron designed by Gustave Eiffel, who later designed the Eiffel Tower. Presented by the French government to the people of the United States, the statue was brought in sections from France and erected on Bedloe's Island in New York Harbor in 1886. The poem written by Emma Lazarus and inscribed on the base of the statue transformed the statue into more than a gesture of friendship between governments. The Statue of Liberty became a symbol of world liberty and of America's destiny—in 1886—as the promised land.

Between the arrival of the statue in 214 wooden crates in June 1885 and its official unveiling in October 1886, various sections of it were displayed to the public for a nominal charge as a means of raising money to pay for the construction of the base—America's responsibility. Photographers seem to have been as fascinated by the statue in pieces—from the time the first plaster sections onto which the thin sheets of copper were modeled were built in Paris—as they would ultimately be by the monument itself. It is perhaps appropriate that as America approached maturity, an image symbolizing the nation's identity was found in the Statue of Liberty. As Alice Austen photographed individually the inhabitants of what would become the world's most populous city, as though each must be recorded before he or she fused into the modern American population, so the pieces of Miss Liberty were carefully recorded by the camera, at just the chronological point where the nation's identity as the most successful democracy in history was assured. As the nation came together and the image of it as the melting pot of nationalities assumed a reality, so were the pieces of the statue welded into the mighty figure dominating the harbor.

The symbol of America as the promised land came to New York harbor in 1886 with the erection of the Statue of Liberty. Designed by Frédéric Bartholdi, the statue was completely dismantled in 1884 after it had been erected in Bartholdi's Paris studio and shipped to Bedloe's Island in New York harbor. Re–erected in October 1886, the statue was said by a later chronicler to give "scale and meaning to the vast open space of the harbor." Here, the plaster hand that will hold the torch is shaped in Bartholdi's workshop.

The face of the statue, here brooding on Bedloe's Island (left), was modeled by Bartholdi on the face of his mistress. American public opinion forced him to marry her when she accompanied Bartholdi on a trip to New York in 1876. The size of the statue becomes more impressive when compared to the adult dwarfed by the lady's crown and toes (below).

France donated the statue, but America had to build the base. To raise the money for the base, the head was set up in New York in 1885 (right), and admission was charged to see it.

The statue was unveiled on a foul day of mist and fog. The harbor was choked with excursion steamers, rowboats, ferries, barges, and boats chartered by private groups ranging from the Union League Club to the Woman Suffrage Association. One of the boats had been reserved by the New York Society of Amateur Photographers, and one of the photographers of the official unveiling of the assembled statue was, appropriately enough, Seneca Ray Stoddard, who had come down from Glens Falls. Stoddard felt that to capture truly the image of "Liberty Enlightening the World" the statue should be photographed at night. Some time after the official unveiling, he rigged up a complicated system of magnesium flashes that were detonated by the electrical plant lighting the statue's torch, and, after several false starts and grappling with wind and broken wires, he succeeded in taking the photograph.

Long concerned with the river and its life, its potential and its preservation—and long concerned with photography as a means of preserving the purity of the river, Stoddard in his photograph of the Statue of Liberty had created a symbol of what the river meant. The rays of the statue's lamp illuminated a path that led—not, as Henry Hudson had hoped, to the riches of the Orient—to the riches of the Future.

Seneca Ray Stoddard descended the river from Glens Falls to make a rare night time shot (right) of the completed statue, using *blitzlichtpulver*—flashlight powder invented in Germany in 1887. *The Brooklyn Citizen* for Feb. 10, 1894, said of this photograph that it was the only view of the statue that Bartholdi himself declared to be worthy of the subject.

149 "Liberty Enlightening the World." Copyright 1889, by S. R. Stoddard, Glens Falls, N. Y.

BIBLIOGRAPHY

There are numerous books used in preparing the text for *The Hudson River 1850-1918* that will be of interest to readers who want to explore the subject further.

General Histories and Literary Works

Adams, Arthur, *The Hudson River in Literature: An Anthology* (State University of New York Press, 1980).

Bacon, Edgar Mayhew, *The Hudson River from Ocean to Source* (G. Putnam's Sons, 1902).

Brown, Henry Collins, *The Lordly Hudson* (Charles Scribner's Sons, 1937).

Carmer, Carl, *The Hudson River* (Holt, Rinehart and Winston, 1939, 1974).

Fink, William B., *Getting to Know the Hudson River* (Coward, 1970).

Greene, Nelson, *History of the Valley of the Hudson* (S. J. Clarke Publishing Company, 1931).

James, Henry, *The American Scene* (Indiana University Press, 1905, 1968).

Johnson, Clifton, *The Picturesque Hudson* (The Macmillan Company, 1909).

Keller, Alan, *Life Along the Hudson* (Sleepy Hollow Press, 1976).

Lossing, Benson, *The Hudson: From the Wilderness to the Sea* (Virtue and Company, 1868, reprinted by Kennikat, 1972).

Reed, John, *The Hudson River Valley* (C. N. Potter, 1960).

Taintor, Charles Newhall, *The Hudson River Route* (Taintor Brothers and Company, 1883).

Van Zandt, Roland, *Chronicles of the Hudson: Three Centuries of Travelers' Accounts* (Rutgers University Press, 1971).

Wilstach, Paul, *Hudson River Landings* (Friedman, 1933)

The Water and River Traffic

Boyle, Robert, *The Hudson River: A Natural and Unnatural History* (Norton, 1969).

Buckman, David Lear, *Old Steamboat Days on the Hudson River* (Gale, 1909).

Burroughs, John, "Our River," *Scribners Magazine*, August, 1880.

Glunt, Ruth Reynolds, *The Old Lighthouses of the Hudson River* (Moran Printing Company, 1969).

Mylod, John, *Biography of a River* (Hawthorn Books, 1969).

New York State Hudson River Valley Commission, *The Hudson* (Published by the compilers, 1966).

Ringwald, Donald C., *Hudson River Day Line* (Howell-North, 1965).

Verplanck, William, *The Sloops of the Hudson* (G. P. Putnam's Sons, 1908).

The Adirondacks

Carson, Russell, *Peaks and People of the Adirondacks* (Adirondack Mountain Club, 1927).

Donaldson, Alfred, *A History of the Adirondacks* (The Century Company, 1921).

Durant, Kenneth, *Guide-Boat Days and Ways* (Syracuse University Press, 1963).

Early, Eleanor, *Adirondack Tales* (Little, Brown and Company, 1939).

Hochschild, Harold, *Life and Leisure in the Adirondack Backwoods* (Syracuse University Press, 1962).

Hooker, Mildred Phelps, *Camp Chronicles* (Adirondack Museum, 1964).

Stoddard, Seneca Ray, *The Adirondacks* (Published by the author, 1893).

Warner, Charles Dudley, *In the Wilderness* (R. West, 1878).

White, William Chapman, *Just About Everything in the Adirondacks* (Syracuse University Press, 1960).

Small Town Life

Gloversville Chamber of Commerce, *Yesterday and Today, Gloversville* (Published by the compilers, 1940).

Hayner, Rutherford, *Troy and Rensselaer County* (Lewis Historical Publishing Company, Inc., 1925).

Howell, William Thompson, *The Hudson Highlands* (Lenz and Riecker, Inc., 1933).

Hyde, Louis Fiske, *History of Glens Falls, New York* (Privately printed, 1936).

Mason, Howard C., *Backward Glances* (Webster Mimeo Service, Glens Falls, 1965).

Murray, David, *Industrial and Material Progress Illustrated in the History of Albany* (Weed, Parsons and Company, 1880).

Myers, James Thorn, *History of the City of Watervliet 1630-1910* (H. Stowell and Son, 1910).

CREDITS

Jacket: Collection of The Hudson River Museum, Yonkers, New York
Title Page: Library of Congress
p. 5: From the Collection of George S. Bolster, Saratoga Springs, New York
p. 7: Library of Congress
p. 8-9, 12: Photo Courtesy Adirondack Museum
p. 14: Library of Congress
p. 15: Photo Courtesy Adirondack Museum
p. 16, 17, 18-19, 20, 21: Library of Congress
p. 22, 23, 25, 26, 27: Photo Courtesy Adirondack Museum
p. 29, 30-31: From the Collection of George S. Bolster, Saratoga Springs, New York
p. 32-33: Albany Institute of History & Art, Albany, New York
p. 35, 36, 38-39: Glens Falls Historical Society
p. 40: Courtesy Rensselaer County Historical Society
p. 41: Library of Congress
p. 42, 43: Courtesy Rensselaer County Historical Society
p. 44, 45, 46, 47, 48, 49, 50, 51: Albany Institute of History & Art, Albany, New York
p. 52: From the Collection of the Ellenville Public Library & Museum
p. 53: Albany Institute of History & Art, Albany, New York
p. 54: Library of Congress
p. 55: Collection of The Hudson River Museum, Yonkers, New York
p. 56: New York Public Library
p. 57: Courtesy Rensselaer County Historical Society
p. 58-59: Courtesy Franklin D. Roosevelt Library
p. 60: Library of Congress
p. 61: Adriance Memorial Library
p. 62-63: Courtesy of The New-York Historical Society, New York City
p. 64: From the Collection of George S. Bolster, Saratoga Springs, New York
p. 65 (top): Library of Congress
p. 65 (bottom): Courtesy of Sleepy Hollow Restorations
p. 66: Library of Congress
p. 67 (top): Glens Falls Historical Association
p. 67 (bottom): The Staten Island Historical Society, Richmondtown, Staten Island, New York
p. 68: From the Collection of George S. Bolster, Saratoga Springs, New York
p. 69: Albany Institute of History & Art, Albany, New York
p. 70-71: Courtesy Rensselaer County Historical Society
p. 72: Library of Congress
p. 73: From the Collection of George S. Bolster, Saratoga Springs, New York
p. 74-75: Albany Institute of History & Art, Albany, New York
p. 76: Collection of The Hudson River Museum, Yonkers, New York
p. 77 (top): Adriance Memorial Library
p. 77 (bottom): Courtesy Franklin D. Roosevelt Library
p. 78 (both): Courtesy of Richard S. Tefft, Greenwich, New York
p. 79, 80, 81: Collection of The Hudson River Museum, Yonkers, New York
p. 82-83: Glens Falls Historical Association
p. 85: United States Military Academy
p. 86: Library of Congress
p. 88, 90: Museum of American Folk Art
p. 91: From the Collection of George S. Bolster, Saratoga Springs, New York
p. 92: Library of Congress
p. 94, 95, 97: From the Collection of George S. Bolster, Saratoga Springs, New York
p. 98-99: Photograph by Byron. The Byron Collection, Museum of the City of New York
p. 101: Albany Institute of History & Art, Albany, New York
p. 103: Library of Congress
p. 104, 105, 107, 108: United States Military Academy

p. 109: Culver Pictures
p. 110: Courtesy of the Museum of the Ossining Society
p. 111: Library of Congress
p. 113, 114-115, 118-119: Vassar College
p. 120: Library of Congress
p. 121 (top): Courtesy of The New-York Historical Society, New York City
p. 121 (bottom): Library of Congress
p. 123: The Staten Island Historical Society, Richmondtown, Staten Island, New York
p. 125: Albany Institute of History & Art, Albany, New York
p. 126: Courtesy of Sleepy Hollow Restorations
p. 127: Library of Congress
p. 128: Courtesy of the Town of Yorktown Museum, Yorktown Heights, New York
p. 129, 130: The Staten Island Historical Society, Richmondtown, Staten Island, New York
p. 131, 132: Courtesy of Sleepy Hollow Restorations
p. 133: Courtesy Franklin D. Roosevelt Library
p. 134: Katonah Village Improvement Society
p. 135: Library of Congress
p. 136, 137 (both): The National Trust for Historic Preservation
p. 139: Courtesy of The New-York Historical Society, New York City
p. 140, 141: From the Collection of George S. Bolster, Saratoga Springs, New York
p. 142: Courtesy Franklin D. Roosevelt Library
p. 143: Courtesy of Sleepy Hollow Restorations
p. 145, 146 (top): Courtesy Franklin D. Roosevelt Library
p. 146 (bottom): Collection of The Hudson River Museum, Yonkers, New York
p. 149, 150, 151: Courtesy New York State Office of Parks and Recreation, Olana State Historic Site
p. 152-153, 154, 155, 156-157, 159: Library of Congress
p. 161: Courtesy of the Mariners Museum, Newport News, Virginia
p. 162: Courtesy of the New-York Historical Society, New York City
p. 164: Museum of the City of New York
p. 165: Courtesy of The New-York Historical Society, New York City
p. 166: The Staten Island Historical Society, Richmondtown, Staten Island, New York
p. 167: Library of Congress
p. 168-169: Museum of the City of New York
p. 170-171: South Street Seaport Museum
p. 173: Photo by Courtesy Public Roads Administration
p. 174, 175: The Staten Island Historical Society, Richmondtown, Staten Island, New York
p. 176: Courtesy of Sleepy Hollow Restorations
p. 177 (both): Photograph by Byron. The Byron Collection Museum of the City of New York
p. 178, 179, 180: The Staten Island Historical Society, Richmondtown, Staten Island, New York
p. 181: Photograph by Byron. The Byron Collection Museum of the City of New York
p. 182-183: Library of Congress
p. 184: Museum of the City of New York
p. 185: New York Public Library
p. 186: The Staten Island Historical Society, Richmondtown, Staten Island, New York
p. 187: Museum of the City of New York
p. 189: Library of Congress
p. 190: Collection of Andrew Spano
p. 191 (both), 193: Library of Congress

ACKNOWLEDGEMENTS

The compiling and editing of a book of photographs necessarily involves the cooperation of many professional and knowledgeable archivists, editors, and collectors. The author would like to thank: Craig A. Gilborn and William Crowley of the Adirondack Museum; Norman Rice and James Hoban of the Albany Institute of History and Art; Joseph King and M. Joan Youngken of the Glens Falls Historical Association; Barbara Hammond of the Hudson River Museum; Jerry Kearns of the Library of Congress; Nancy Richards of Lyndhurst; James Ryan of Olana; Mrs. Frederick Walsh and Stacy Pomeroy of the Rensselaer County Historical Society; Raymond Teichman of the Franklin Delano Roosevelt Library at Hyde Park; Norman Brouwer of the South Street Seaport Museum; Charles Sachs and Barnett Shepherd of the Staten Island Historical Society; and Frances Goudy of Vassar College. The photographic researchers who participated in this project were continually enthusiastic and made significant contributions: Diane Hamilton, Enid Klass, Ruth Schindler, and M. Joan Youngken. The interest and encouragement of Saverio Procario and James Gullickson of Sleepy Hollow Restorations were greatly appreciated.

The author is particularly grateful to Stephen Elliott of Sachem Publications for his intelligent editing and his patience and to Susan Elliott for her moral support and her hospitality.

INDEX

Page number references appearing in italics refer to photographs and captions.